Memories of Mexico and Recipes, too

by Dorothy Weeks

photographs by Lowell Weeks

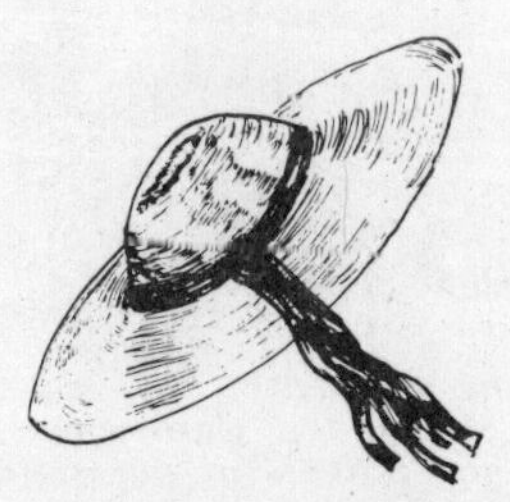

a México, lindo y querido

TITLES IN THE MINUTIAE MEXICANA SERIES

A Flower Lover's Guide to Mexico
A Bird Watcher's Guide to Mexico
A Guide to Mexican Archaeology
A Guide to Mexican Witchcraft
A Guide to Mexican History
A Guide to Tequila, Mezcal and Pulque
A Guide to Mexican Poetry, Ancient and Modern
A Guide to Architecture in Ancient Mexico
A Guide to Mexican Ceramics
Minute Guide to Speaking Spanish

INDIAN PEOPLES OF MEXICO SERIES

The Maya World
The Aztecs, Then and Now

PERSONAL ADVENTURE SERIES

Not as a Tourist . . . in Mexico
Memories of Mexico, and Recipes, Too

Derechos reservados conforme a la ley © 1983

ISBN 968-7074-10-8

Editorial MINUTIAE MEXICANA, S. A. de C. V.
Insurgentes Centro 114-210; 06030 México, D. F.;
Tel. 535-9488

There are many representations of Quetzalcoatl, a god ancient in Middle America before the Christian era began. We have adopted as the insignia of our series the most common — that of the feathered serpent. The father and creator of man, Quetzalcoatl was the beneficent god of life and the wind, the god of civilization who inspired man to study the stars, to develop agriculture, industry and the arts.

Impreso y hecho en México

FOREWORD

Dorothy, with her diary, and Lowell Weeks, with his camera, have traveled the world over — a month-long safari in Africa, two weeks on a houseboat in Kashmir, a freighter run through Micronesia, Tibet, the Near and the Far East, Europe. But it has been to Mexico that they have returned most frequently through the years, to Dorothy's *México lindo y querido* of three decades past which Lowell recorded on film with such warm feeling for the country and its people.

The Weeks made their first trip to Mexico in 1947. The last visit recorded in this book is that to Veracruz in 1958. Most of the photographs reproduced in the following pages were printed shortly after being taken, and the negatives no longer exist so they have the true patina of time. Lowell has won several prestigious prizes for his photographs, has been published in such magazines as Saturday Review of Literature, National Geographic, Southland, MEXICO/ This Month, and furnished the cover shot for the book "Around the World in 1,000 Pictures." He had a one-man show in Chicago sponsored by a Mexican airline, and his pictures are in the permanent collection of the Long Beach (California) Museum of Arts.

On her return from any trip, Dorothy heads for her kitchen to reconstruct outstanding dishes from that particular jaunt before the memory of flavor and aroma is gone. In the course of that exercise, she may make some adaptations, for what dedicated cook can resist changing, adding to or subtracting from a recipe. Such inventiveness may be the result of personal preferences, or the unavailability of a particular ingredient, or simply because the flavor *might* be improved. Witness such triumphs as her "Incredible Pork Roast," "Wild Lime Pie," and her many tequila "invents."

Dorothy, like most very good cooks, operates by instinct, until the creation in question looks, feels, smells and/or tastes right. To translate a pinch of this or a handful of that into cups and ounces took a little doing. There was considerable across-the-border kibbitzing with her editor plus several extra pounds acquired by Dorothy and very willing volunteer friends (Lowell is a steak-and-potatoes man) in the course of testing.

It must be understood that the recipes given herein are, in many cases, not the versions laboriously concocted in Mexican kitchens. Dorothy Weeks has simplified, yet conserved the essence of many Mexican dishes so that you may savor the taste of Mexico without much of the work.

The Publishers

TABLE OF CONTENTS

Drawings by B. B. Hutchinson

Pasteup: Román Padilla

Cover: San Miguel de Allende. A black and white version of this photograph won the first prize (a trip to Europe) for Lowell Weeks in a *Saturday Review of Literature* contest. In the middle distance rises the landmark of San Miguel, the parish church. The exterior, with its neo-Gothic spires was executed by Zeferino Gutiérrez, an architect who lacked formal academic training, in the late 19th century, and has been a favorite subject for photographers since then.

Lowell asked these two lads to climb the hill with us for a bird's-eye view of colonial Alamos. Right center is the church with the dinner plates in the tower. On a visit to that church a priest asked me to leave! I was wearing a thin, short-sleeved linen blouse — shame on me!

AMIGOS EN ALAMOS

The barren mountains shrouded in purple haze that surround Alamos probably looked the same to Conquistador Francisco Vázquez de Coronado as they did to us on our arrival, 411 years later. Vázquez de Coronado departed Alamos in 1540 on his way north to search for the fabled cities of Cíbola. We arrived in Alamos in May, 1951 for a quiet vacation.

During its 19th-century silver-mining heyday, the population of Alamos, Sonora reached 35,000 but in 1951, the mines closed and the inhabitants reduced to a mere 3,000, Alamos was a tranquil village and just what we were looking for.

We had written Señorita Emelia Almada and she graciously accepted us as guests in her home. She was witty and charming, and our Spanish and her English provoked many laughs. A descendant of the Almada family noted in local history, she told us of one of her ancestors who ordered a path of silver "tiles" laid from his mansion to the church door so that his daughter would not walk to her wedding in the dust. We didn't walk in dust, or silver, at her house, but we did dodge cats and chickens every day. Noting our acrobatics, Señorita Almada observed, "Bery oglies, my cats, but bery high class my shikens." Yes, the cats were ugly but I could make no comment on the chickens since I'm not up on social distinction in poultry circles.

There were other guests at the Almada home, among them a widow, sixtyish, who was booked to sail shortly thereafter on a world cruise. While reading the ship brochure one morning she told me that bar drinks at sea were only 14 cents each. "I think I will try them all at that price," she said, "even though I have never had a drink." It sounded like an invitation to chaos and I hope she survived.

Our first morning in town introduced us to what was to become a daily pattern. Church bells rang the call to mass at daybreak. Then the air was lively with the mixed strains of enthusiastic roosters, bark-

Victoria at her early morning chore. I did not fully appreciate those fresh tortillas then, but I certainly would now.

ing dogs, the jingling of bells hanging from burros' necks and the clop-clop of their feet on the cobblestone street.

In our *casa* there was much activity. The early arrival of Victoria the maid and María the cook was followed by special smells and sounds: the fragrance of an open fire and the aroma of bubbling coffee; then the pat-pat of dextrous brown hands shaping the day's tortillas, accompanied by soft laughter and musical conversations in Spanish. Breakfasts were gay affairs in the mellow sunlight of the patio. We had our choice of pineapple, mango, papaya or bananas, followed by *huevos rancheros* (the eggs supplied by those highbrow shikens), spicy *chorizo, pan dulce* warm from the nearby baker's oven and, if you were still hollow, hot cakes with honey right out of the hive.

Early on in our stay we inquired about a garage and gasoline. Our search ended under the branches of a huge tree. No building, just a fenced enclosure, gentle breezes and warm sunshine. A rusted engine rested on a trestle and scattered about indiscriminately were other car parts. Gasoline was brought in by truck from Navajoa in 55-gallon drums and the requested amount was slowly poured in the tank by means of a small tin can. This method was a lesson in patience and optimism.

Through our wanderings as the days passed, and with the help of Señorita Almada, we were introduced to the town's history, its points of interest, and inhabitants. One day a short walk took us to an hacienda, a charming place with spacious rooms, patios and graceful colonnades. Certainly the bathroom was the only one of its kind. On the wall behind the stone tub was an oil painting — a view of bathing beauties and mustachioed gentlemen in the plunge at Venice, California, circa 1900. As a young man, the owner had visited Venice and returned home with a colored postcard of the plunge. An artist friend reproduced the scene on the bathroom wall so that while the Don kept himself clean he could keep his memory green.

There are many such elegant homes, or their ruins, in Alamos

A daily gathering under the tremendous trees in the Alameda. Where are the women? Working, what else?

since it was once the greatest silver-mining center in New Spain. Silver was discovered in 1683 and opulent prosperity continued until the end of the 19th century when the mines were worked out. Alamos even had its own mint from 1864-69, and its economic importance determined that it should be the capital of the State of El Occidente from 1827 until 1831 when the area was divided into the present-day states of Sonora and Sinaloa.

Norteamericanos began arriving in Alamos in the late 1940's, some of the first being prospectors smitten by visions of extracting silver from the old mines. Those that we met though were near-to-retirement or retired people, seeking a more elegant lifestyle. Even in this, Alamos is unique. There is no "foreign" residential district; the homes of the newcomers are scattered throughout the town, wherever they found a house (or ruin) to their liking. Restoration

Señor Hernández, the "Jumping Bean King," and partner. Actions speak louder than words, to coin a phrase.

Our Theater. That is the back of my head, front row left. Those seats were not too comfortable but the situation and the movie more than compensated.

outside was in the colonial style but changes occurred within — bathrooms were moved inside, and kitchens were transformed. Electric equipment replaced charcoal or wood stoves and gleaming refrigerators hummed. We wondered what the ghost of an 18th-century Indian servant would think if she chanced upon such shining splendor.

Our favorite observation points were the Alameda, a park shaded by giant *alamos* or cottonwood trees, and the small commercial center, where we watched sandaled Indians, market-bound with their heavy loads, small children carrying cans of water, stray pigs disturbing the dirt, shabby widows in black clothes resting on the benches, and patient burros waiting for their masters who were delivering wood or visiting the cantina.

Another vantage point was the more stately Plaza de Armas with its planting of royal palms. We had been told to look at the decoration on the tower of the parochial church: china dinner plates. At the time of the church's construction (1786-1804), decorative tile was not available so the wealthy women of Alamos donated plates from their best dinner services. Only a few plates remained, most having been shattered when they served as bull's-eyes for restless soldiers. The

If your visit is coming to an end, and in the clear sunny air of Alamos the buildings sparkle, it is time to capture just one more picture...

most interesting of Alamo's *portales* or arcades stands to the west of the church. Behind the arcades are attractive homes, their windows and facades adorned with the wrought-iron work for which the town is famous. Sometimes we caught tempting glimpses of fountains and flowers when doors were ajar.

Shopping tours with Señorita Almada were not to be missed. We visited many places: to the beekeeper (Chinese) for honey; to a store for corn; to another for a new frying pan; to still another for *panocha* (brown sugar cones), and to yet another for a made to order embroidered skirt. Then on to watch the skillful fingers of the little basketmaker weave the tules brought up from the river's edge. The town potter, only 24 years of age, had been making the town's supply of *ollas, cazuelas* and *comales* since he was 12. Further on, a small red flag fluttering above a doorway told us fresh meat was available.

One night a week we went to the movie under the stars in the courtyard of the Alamos hotel. Chairs were placed wherever you chose to sit. Cost? nine pesos for four people. One title I recall was *Matrimonio y Mortaja* (Matrimony and Shroud), but I do not remember the story, fortunately. The sound system was adjusted for the benefit of the people in Navajoa, 30 miles away.

One evening a dance was held at the hotel in honor of visiting norteamericanos. The highlight of the festivity was the dancing of a Señor Hernández, known to the locals as the "Jumping-bean King" for his dealings in that commodity. My diary says we had rum and cake at home to complete the evening.. This I do not remember either. I was hypnotized by the *brincos* of the King of the *Frijoles Brincadores*.

Another evening we waltzed ourselves over to the plaza to enjoy the promenade, complete with serenata. Girls, arm in arm, strolled in one direction around the kiosk bandstand; boys draggled the other way. We were told this is a very old Mexican custom.

Shortly after we returned home, we read that Alamos had been proclaimed a Colonial Monument, which means that all restoration must be done in the colonial style and new construction must conform to that period. In any case, it has remained in our memory as a monument to tranquil, gracious living, an oasis of serenity only 470 miles south of the U.S. border.

The "snake charmer," me and my boa in the court-yard of Hotel Belmar. He'd been reclining on the bar just before this episode. *Photo Michele McMillan*

Between my diary and my memory (I don't tell my diary every-thing), this is Mazatlán as we saw it some 30 years ago.

We climbed aboard a Mexicana plane in Tijuana, B.C. and bounced down in jig, or is it jug time? Tranquilized on orange juice and tequila, relaxed and in the mood to celebrate the New Year, we were welcomed once more at the Hotel Belmar on Olas Altas Bay. On our agenda was time in the "old rockin' chairs" in the patio and galería, and they soon got us.

Rocking and savoring icy cold Dos Equis beer we reminisced of previous Mazatlán vacations... Of the time I helped untangle the boa from the chairs in the courtyard where it was sunning. The snake lived in the basement and kept the hotel free of vermin... Of the morning we took a launch to one of the offshore islands to drink fresh coconut milk. A friend, the same one with us this time, tried to imitate the native boys and show us how he too could chop off a coconut top with a machete. He did, and lost a slice of thumb... Of the days we rode with Napoleón in his horse-drawn carriage with "the fringe on top." I recalled my tours with Pancho in his taxi. He exuberantly knew where to find "anythings." He knew the jail held "murders, crimers and stillers." And that the ghostly old ruin on the hill "burned with thunder lightnings." This is heady information, and I'll always cherish the day he asked me for the English words to "Alice Blue Nightgown."

We sat till the sun dropped into the ocean, then climbed the stairs to dress for the New Year's ball that very night. The orchestra blasted merrily till dawn, but we gave up after a sinfully excellent midnight dinner, and fell into bed. We had had a full day in more ways than one.

After a restorative breakfast of fresh pineapple, panqués, steak, frijoles, and *iced* coffee, we made sword-fishing plans at the pier, and then went to town (my idea). I've spent hours and days shopping in Mexico and it will never lose its fascination. Between the *tiendas* and the stalls at the market, and around the plaza, I am in the groove. These are the moments when my husband wonders why he said "I do" or maybe it was "I will." It was always "What in God's name is that?" or, frigidly, "May I ask how you intend to get this home?"

After this spree, limp as the fringe on a lamp and overloaded with

Mazatlán, as taken from near the jail which held the "crimers and stillers."

Two proud and smelly sportsmen with the day's catch.

irrestibles (mine) we collapsed at a *Comedor Familiar*. We had liberal helpings of lentil soup, crusty *bolillos,* carrots with lime juice and sugar, *carne asada,* abalone, scrambled eggs with chorizo, tortillas, ice cold beer (again), and tonic water. That last item to keep us physically fit for the fight with the marlin waiting out there in the blue Pacific (I think positive). If you've been paying attention you can see right away why the spirit didn't move us to do anything acrobatic after that lunch so we lolled around.

Happy fishing day came. We ate a hearty breakfast (seems we are always eating doesn't it?): frijoles with fresh *cilantro,* scrambled eggs with tomatoes and chiles, hot tortillas, and frosty beer, and off we trotted to the pier.

We were three ecstatic and expectant gringos totally ignorant of deep sea fishing who put ourselves into the capable hands of Tomás and Gregorio, the young skippers of the motorboat. It was "into the boat, men," as the engine revved up and we scudded out to sea. Rods in sockets, bait skipping behind, instructions were given to "keep your seat and watch for black tails cutting the water like knives." All was serene and peaceful and I was quietly singing (I thought) *All Alone*. After a few bars the man in my life wryly observed he'd rather I was, and just at that moment we heard beautiful music. A line snapped, a reel spun, and in the commotion Gregorio shouted, "Eet's a mar-leen!" Lowell had first dibs so he jumped into the chair. Tomás buckled the harness, shoved the pole into his hands while the reel yowled and screeched, and we had our first glimpse of glistening black beauty. The fish pulled, leaped and lunged. Some-

The strange, multistyle Cathedral of Mazatlán. In Mexico, cathedrals, as the seats of bishoprics, are usually in state capitals. This one is an exception.

The New Year's Ball held in the dining room of the Hotel Belmar. Those Mexican belles were *muy elegantes*.

times he walked on his tail across the water, sometimes he sounded. When he did that the boys said he was lying below sulking. Sometimes, like a streak of lightning, he would shoot up from the depths in a torrent of water, lashing his head back and forth in a mad frenzy to throw the hook. Repeatedly he struggled, but finally exhausted he was slowly reeled in and floated alongside. Tomás was on the spot with his gaff, and the boys pulled the huge fish aboard. All silvery and iridescent blue he lay there, tied to the deck. Then a second line was readied and our friend reeled in marlin number two.

Mid-afternoon brought wind and choppy water so we headed for the mainland. Our boys made their one and only goof. We came in at the Yacht Club (loose term). That meant a ride to the hoist where catches are racked up and fishermen stand by for photographs. We rattled across town in a prehistoric taxi with two smelly marlin and three smelly people. Make that four, I'll include the driver. My husband commented on the gamy odor and our friend, who was bleary with a head cold, said he wished he could smell. We told him not to worry, he did. At the Mazatlán hoist the marlins were suspended, the sportsmen proudly posed and pictures taken. Weight of fish, 193 and 186 lbs. For first timers it was a glorious adventure. Don't ask me what pound test line was used. I think that's the term. For all I know it could have been lasso size. And the catch? We gave those mar-leens to the lads hanging around the dock.

In our allotted two weeks we went to the familiar places and added some new ones. For instance, we made a morning call at a sugar mill and watched barefooted men sweep sugar through holes in the floor into boxes below, ready for shipping. Does that stretch your mind? We toured a brewery and watched that excellent brew in the making, necessitating a fast walk to the nearest cantina. Pancho took me again to the Mercado Central for *huaraches,* the sandals which have lent wings to my feet all over Mexico. Only 64 cents U.S. a pair in those days, beautifully made and all leather.

We couldn't overlook Café Inez up on the hill to the left of our hotel, and decided to give it a try. We entered, sat down and waited, and waited, and waited. Nothing happened so we left but on reaching the street a male voice behind us inquired if we wished dinner and if so, would we please return. "I am the owner, my girls do not have the English and were afraid to speak with you. Tonight we serve wild pig and wild lime pie." Pig and pie, who-wee!!! Do I have to tell you we toasted the Señor with our wine and left in a blissful state. No beer tonight.

Playtime was fast disappearing but we still had a fiesta in our future. The new governor of the state of Sinaloa was being honored with a parade and carnival, right in front of our hotel. Decorated booths, garlands of paper flowers, food stalls, señoras and señoritas in lacy gowns, handsome *charros* in costume, *mariachis* distinctive in black and silver, and fireworks. After a tumultuous fanfare the governor gave a spirited speech, people cheered, girls danced, horses pranced, silver spurs jingled, trumpeters pierced the air, fireworks burst and rockets exploded. We observed this from our second floor balcony, drinking our beer, making flowery speeches, and waving graciously to the celebrants below as we sprinkled them with flower petals. Alas, we were unnoticed. Farewell, Mazatlán.

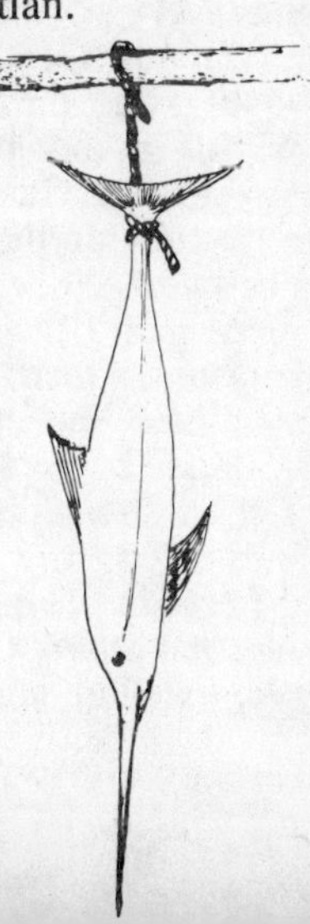

A GLIMPSE OF GUANAJUATO

Seduced by the charm of Mexico we returned year after year, like the swallows to Capistrano. Guanajuato was our destination in June 1952. The city lies in a narrow valley, enclosed by rich ore-bearing, rugged hills covered with cacti, rocks and scrub, about 260 miles northwest of Mexico City.

Our guidebook predicted that ghosts of the past lurk around every corner and on every hill. A few would be fine but we didn't care to encounter too many. After checking in at our hotel we walked to the Alhóndiga (granary) of Granaditas. If specters haunt the granary, we didn't see them but we did listen to a tragic story. The cages hanging from iron hooks at the four corners of the building roof once held the heads of Father Hidalgo and his aides, those inspired men who defied the Spaniards and, on a hill overlooking the city, is the pink stone statue of Pípila, another of the heroes in that bloody struggle for independence from Spain. The monument commemorates the bravery of the young man who stormed and fired the door of the Alhóndiga, and it bears a fiery inscription: "There are still other alhóndigas to burn."

Vivid in memory is the visit to the *panteón* (cemetery), the catacombs of Guanajuato. The custodian told us that something in the dry air, or the clay, preserves the dead. We descended a spiral stairway to the vault below and there, rows of mummified bodies leaned against the walls, grotesque and gruesome. Some were clothed, others not. Once when we showed Lowell's slides to a friend from Guanajuato she cried, "Oh, there's Señor. . . the watchmaker!" He was dressed.

On La Presa de los Santos ("the Saints' Dam," no longer in use) stands a long row of broken stone figures. It was a very sorry sight, but I couldn't help thinking of Louis Armstrong and his joyous music, *When the Saints Come Marchin' In.*

We toiled up a hill to see the fabulous Valenciana mine and church.

The same guidebook reported that the silver from this mine overflowed the coffers of Phillip II for many years. The circular opening of the mine is 30 feet across and 1,600 feet in depth. A caretaker's child, playing in the debris, threw a large stone down the shaft for our benefit(?). Seconds elapsed and then a whooshing, whistling thunderous rumble exploded with a roar. It was two days before we could hear properly. A friend, a North American who was born in Guanajuato, said when the mine was producing and the lift went down to bring the miners to the surface, the first ones began to sing, and as each group got on, they too sang, and so on to the top, their song floating up to the families waiting above ground. In our opinion, those miners surely qualified for heaven. Lowell asked me to stand just at the edge of the abyss; he needed a figure in the picture. I declined. I am not a heroine, just a certified coward.

The Valenciana church on the same hill is rich in history and ornamentation. Did I believe the story that the mortar used in the building was mixed with powdered gold and silver and Spanish wine? Well... maybe. We peered into the windows of the past at the magnificent home of the Conde de Rul, owner of the mine and builder of the church. Past glories of colonial Mexico.

Our first hotel was the Orozco, our second the newly opened

The aqueduct in Guanajuato, ancient and crumbling.

Valenciana Church, in need of restoration. Much still needs to be done in this respect to preserve this and other gems of Mexico.

Castillo de Santa Cecilia, a real castle with crenelated towers and parapets, on a hill overlooking the city. We were among the first guests and a year later at a reunion, Salvador, the manager gave us an iron replica of the key to the portal door, and a scroll enclosed in a wooden cylinder. That word reminds me of *cilindros* (street organs). In the evenings you could hear their sweet and poignant melodies. I almost forgot to say we had square pillows on the beds at Santa Cecilia. For squareheads? You can see I'm thinking.

The timeworn road leading from town to the hotel was like a page from a storybook. Low crumbling bridges were just wide enough for burros or people, but not both together, and adobe homes painted in soft pinks, yellow and blues lined the road on either side. Flowers

spilled from windows, and bird cages with their singing captives hung from pegs in the walls. Our favorite spot along this pathway was the Café Venta Viaje San Javier. It was a great place for a beer, and I quote below the epigrams lettered on one wall:

Si el agua destruye los caminos	If water destroys roads
Qué hará con los intestinos!!	What will it do to intestines!!
and	
El agua es obra del poder Divino	Water is the work of the Lord
Y el vino es obra del poder humano	Wine is the doing of man
Respetamos el agua	Let us respect water
Y consumamos el vino.	And consume wine.

Praise the Lord and pass the ammunition! It was during one stop, while enjoying a foaming tankard with extra hilarity (for we were practicing our deplorable Spanish), a voice belonging to a North American seated nearby pleaded: "Seen-yor, how do you say 'Jimmy Hamilton' in Spanish?"

The inability to communicate gave me some distressful moments once upon a time. We were in the capital and I was in a dither to wear flowers in my pierced ears after the fashion of the stately beauties of Tehuantepec. Now I couldn't put dirty string in my ears, I had to have something sterile. Say, catgut. That word was not in

That road in Guanajuato which we traveled many times **going** to Hotel Castillo Santa Cecilia, usually stopping at our old inn for a beer.

my dictionary but I found intestines. So I wrote a request, went to the *farmacia,* handed the druggist my slip of paper, and he handed me a length of tubing with a thingamabob on one end. I could only close my eyes and flee. Our Mexican doctor friend came to the hotel that evening and I told him of my blunder. I actually thought he would do what is called "die laughing." Finally he gasped, "Why Dottie, all you had to say was, *"Tiene catgut?"* I got my catgut from him, and have since tried to avoid dithers.

To return to Guanajuato, the Cañón de Marfil down the road a piece gave us another ghost. We were told that it was here, on the very bridge where we stood, that Maximilian kissed Carlota goodbye. He was executed later in Querétaro by a firing squad. Sentimental me, I got a lump in my throat.

I wonder if somewhere in Mexico an old custom still prevails? When the *faroles* or lanterns along the cobblestone streets were lighted and the watchman on the corner blew his whistle, faintly from another corner came an answering whistle, indicating, in the still of the night, all was well.

We found the homes of two famous people on a quiet walk one day: that of Diego Rivera, who was born here, and the one where President Benito Juárez resided for a time. We admired Guanajuato's noted Teatro Juárez where many famous European opera stars have performed. Distinctive pottery is made in this city, and we watched potters at work on San Luisito Street. The red earthenware was tempting but someone at my elbow hastily changed my mind. He remembered lugging onyx home from Puebla.

We visited Querétaro, Dolores Hidalgo, and San Miguel de Allende, all bursting with historical sites, and then there was Celaya where I found *cajeta de Celaya,* a deadly rich carmel spoon candy. It comes in a wooden box and sticks up everything if you're not careful. I was a Grade A glutton. Something besides my cultural horizon always broadens when I travel.

Mulling over memories of this part of Mexico, I recall it was close to election day and Lowell was frisked a number of times. If the authorities were searching for pistols, he hadn't brought his. He thought the Revolution was over.

These lighthearted accounts of a country we love are precious memories. Mexico has been kind, giving us many laughs and many friends. There it lies, inviting us back, south of the border.

Simply a breathtaking night shot of Guanajuato from the Santa Cecilia.

The center of this small corner of the **San Cristobal** market, the social and economic gathering place of the **Indian** groups of the area, was a huge pile of shelled corn, hidden by buyers.

INDIANS OF THE CLOUD LANDS

A picture book Indian had just passed us on the road and behind him walked his docile wife in her somber dress.

Another dream had come true. We were in San Cristóbal de Las Casas where we hoped to photograph some of the people and sights. The town, perched like a bird in a giant rock nest, overlooked a countryside of emerald green glowing with wild flowers — *manto de la Virgen* (morning glory), the pink flower called "lion's paw," the golden mimosa.

To reach San Cristóbal in Chiapas state, we took Highway 190 east from Tehuantepec. The cloud covered highway climbs through dense forests, the home of the legendary and exotic quetzal bird and hundreds of different orchids. Kilometer 1188, seven thousand feet high in the mountains, was our goal and the home of the Indians of the cloud lands. With each kilometer we had driven further into the past.

The natives of the region are of Maya descent, short, shy and unsophisticated. Each group wore the distinctive dress of its own village but the homes, or huts, were all alike. The roofs were thatched with *zacate,* a species of hay-like grass, and reeds, tied in bundles and secured to roof poles with hemp. A hole left at the peak served as a chimney.

Of all the Indians who gathered daily in the marketplace, our favorite was the Zinacanteco male with his jaunty hat and unusual sandals. Reminiscent of the footwear of the ancient Maya, these wooden soled sandals have a wide collar of leather extending up the back of the leg. The higher the leather piece, the higher the social status, it says here in my diary. Bronze, shapely legs showed off to advantage beneath very brief white cotton shorts. Over a long-sleeved shirt, a sleeveless pink and white striped poncho ended in soft fringe at the cuff of his shorts. Over his arm was a woven bag. A checked black and white scarf with three huge shocking-pink tassels draped his neck, and a handwoven *palma* hat, with myriad rainbow colored ribbons cascading over the brim, rode at a jaunty

Here is our Tojolabal, a "diaper Indian," the most photogenic in the rags which he wore with dignity.

angle on his black hair, adding a devil-may-care look to this highland dandy.

His blood brother, the Tojolabal, sometimes known as the "diaper Indian," was nearly as eye-catching with his ribbon decorated hat but, his most important piece of clothing was his version of the familiar three-cornered baby garment.

The very reserved Indians of San Andrés Chamula were less handsome in dress; they belted knee-length black and white wool *jorongos* at the waist. Sandals were similar to huaraches and though they wear the same type of woven hats, the ribbons are of modest coffee brown leather. Some of the Chamula males distinguish themselves by adding deep red cuffs to their shirts.

The men of all the villages wove palma hats, using 12 strands at a time in an intricate method of braiding. They wove incessantly any place, any time — as they walked along the road, visited at the market or sat on the ground at home. The color of the ribbons tied just so on the hat indicated the status, whether the wearer was a jaunty bachelor or a less waggish married man.

In direct contrast to the theatrical males, the women of the region appeared drab and dispirited. With tousled hair, faded cotton blouses,

dark homespun ankle length skirts, they carried heavy burdens and/or babies on their backs and trotted about barefooted.

One day when my husband received permission to photograph a particular "Mariano," the man called to his wife for his scarf with the pink tassels. He draped it around his shoulders, faced the camera stoically and continued to weave. Evidently the ensemble must be correct for these fashion plates of Chiapas. (Every male to whom we spoke was named "Mariano.")

The market in San Cristóbal sat high above the street with stone steps leading upward on three sides and on top, confusion and clutter. Corn, beans, fruit, meat, salt, pans, dogs, clay pots, and wood crowded every inch of space. The Indians laughed, talked, and pointed at us as we took pictures. Aside from the bustle of the market, the general atmosphere of the town was lazy. Maybe I should say, slow.

We remember how cold it was at night but we were happy at our hotel, the Español. Under the thoughtful supervision of the owner Señor Valeriano Lobeira C., we had all the hot water we wished, comfortable beds, a fine shower, and a fireplace. Food, excellent! beef, good coffee and chocolate, pan dulce, rich hot soup, and impeccable service. Señor Lobeira had eight children and two of

The Indians here were fascinated with Lowell's big camera and this one did not know it was his turn to be photographed.

the sons waited table. One breakfast was particularly hilarious. A hen, destined for the stew pot, called on us that morning, and we had a wild time as Señor Lobeira's octet pursued the reluctant hen through rooms and patios. Room and meals for two were 54 pesos a day. That was $4.32 U.S.

We are indebted to Señor Lobeira for information on San Cristóbal, which has a wealth of treasures dating from the colonial period. The ancient churches, Cathedral, and convents were in good repair, along with a mill constructed in 1546 by Dominican monks. And your imagination would be stimulated by the region around San Cristóbal for it is threaded with archaeological dreams. To the north, among many others, are fabulous Palenque, Yaxchilán, and jungle-shackled Bonampak. Close to San Cristóbal were the Maya ruins of Moshviquil being excavated by archaeologist Frans Blom and his wife Gertrudis, a fascinating couple who showed us around their home and museum.

This was strange and mysterious country to our Tarascan friend and guide Rafael Aldeco, as it was to us, and he had been giving it some serious thought. One day, indicating a group of Indians at the market, Rafael remarked, "Do you think these people care who is president of Mexico or what is going on outside their small community? These people live now. The past and future are of no importance. Time, as we know it, does not exist for them. They live in the clouds."

A happy Chamula who was anxious to have his picture taken and followed Lowell trying to get into each snap of the shutter.

From the open-air living room of a friend, a view of the rooftops of Puerto Vallarta, the Cuale River, and Banderas Bay.

PASSAGE TO
PUERTO VALLARTA - 1957

We had an adventure. It started with us getting on a bus in Mazatlán to go to Tepic (where we were to catch a plane to Puerto Vallarta), with our seven pieces of luggage. And wouldn't you know! a couple of hours out of Mazatlán the bus sat down on its hind legs and expired. I expected the *chofer* to tune up a handy piston rod he just happened to have around and away we'd go. But no. We were stuck.

We milled around with our fellow travelers (people, babies, and dogs) on that hillside for some time before the driver gave up and suggested we catch another bus, any bus. That was easy for the other travelers. They had only small sacks or cloth bundles and were used to hanging on busses by their eyelashes. We didn't know any tricks and besides WE had SEVEN pieces of luggage. So there we were, and it got later and later and we got tired-er and tired-er. Once I made a short climb up the hillside and returned. Then my roomate went, and returning asked if I had seen the dinner plate size toads. HOP TOADS! If one had touched me I would have been in Tepic without benefit of bus.

Buses came by all right, but they were filled to overflowing. They did, however, stop and offer help. Sometimes one or two of our cluster found a toe hold and took off. We sat awhile and stood awhile and wondered and wandered and wallowed in our misery. Finally it got dark, black dark, and we watched the stars come out and dreamed of the comforts of home. But we had our spirits lifted momentarily when one of our bunch started playing an accordion and what do you think he played? "The Poor People of Paris." *Dios mío,* it was funnier than the night in Oaxaca when the marimba band in the plaza played "I Can't Tell a Waltz from a Tango."

Well, 20 buses and 147 mosquito bites later we were scooped and shoved, along with our luggage, into a bus and at 2:30 a.m. crawled into bed at the Sierra de Alica Hotel in Tepic. And at 5:30 a.m. we were jerked straight up in bed, glassy-eyed. A full army band was playing reveille right under our windows, horns blasting, drums rat-

THE bridge over the Cuale in 1957.

a-tat-tat BOOM, and soldiers, a whole regiment clomp-clomp-clomp-ing on the cobblestones. Staggered as I was, I had the insane desire to throw open the window and make like Barbara Fritchie.

We were certainly wide awake now, so we pulled ourselves together and went out to see about plane tickets to Puerto Vallarta, and as quickly came unglued again. The plane was no bigger than your Uncle John's derby! a Cessna, piloted by a Captain Fierro. Fare: $15.36 U.S., round trip for two. We weighed in with our luggage and away we went over the mountains. Thirty minutes later we made a credible landing in a fenceless field, there being no air strip. That was 1957, remember? Almost hidden in the luxuriant weeds was one battered but determined taxi, our Rocinante. We rattled into town on that serene and dewy morning and drew up in front of our ocean front hotel — El Paraíso (Paradise!). Signs advised us that it was the "best and most modern on the coast of Jalisco," and that we had *moralidad absoluta,* a state of grace available then. Another plug for our hotel, especially in view of prevailing conditions in P.V. today, was the price: room and meals for two, $7.20 U.S. per day.

After a breakfast of fresh pineapple, *huevos rancheros, frijoles refritos,* and *café con leche,* we slept, exhausted. Our room was on the second floor, looking up the hill and out toward the river, with a view of the ocean from the other end of our balcony. Our bathroom was something special. It was about three feet square, and the shower head came out of the wall right over the basin and toilet. A shower practically any time you entered.

Late morning we made our first trip to the beach, traversing the swing-and-sway suspension bridge over the Cuale River. The Pacific was never more blue or soft and the swimming was wonderful! A fast pass through town and we were back at the hotel for siesta time, accompanied by a gorgeous tropical thunderstorm. That first night we found that three of our fellow countrymen were also staying in Paradise — two from Beverly Hills and one from Berkeley. P.V. wasn't what you'd call busy. I guess there were no more than 10 "foreigners" in town. We turned in early and noted thankfully: NO insects.

Seventeen days of serenity in Puerto Vallarta. We spent a lot of time down by the river watching the women wash clothes, bathe their children or themselves in the bright sparkling water. Or we just watched the traffic flow across that suspension bridge (foot traffic only) over the Cuale. One misstep and you were in the river.

We either walked or rode to the beach which was across the river and down the coast — the one in front of the hotel was simply rocks and boulders. Down there we swam or sat under palm thatched *palapas* and had *refrescos* or *cervezas*. Sometimes young lads broiled fish for us over driftwood fires. Occasionally we could see men out in the surf unloading bananas brought from the hillsides up Cabo Corrientes way.

One day we took a launch to Yelapa with the aforementioned

Strolls around the village paid off in local color. Here one phase of village life.

This view from our launch the day we went to Yelapa reminded us of lazy days in the South Pacific.

Californians. It took all day to get there and back with a visit to the waterfall thrown in. The coastline looked like Lowell's pictures of Polynesia with the palm thatched houses, banana groves, and brown skinned natives. The climb to the waterfall was rugged, over rocks, and tree trunks laid across small gorges, but it was worth the trip. We saw two boas, one deer (or was it a large dog?), lots of orchids and parrots. The man who took us to the falls invited us to sit under his shade trees and rest when we returned, and gave us each a banana. They tasted so good Lowell wanted to buy a few. But, he couldn't buy a few; the man would sell nothing but the whole stalk (32 cents) and so for several days our balcony was perfumed with bananas.

On our last evening we walked around the plaza, bought fruit and candy at the little stores, listened to the mariachis playing in the *cantinas,* went to the Oceano Hotel for cocktails and dinner, and enjoyed a thunderstorm. Water poured down in torrents in the middle of the open patio but we were high and dry at one side.

The next morning our small Cessna arrived and again we were the only passengers. Courteous and accommodating, Captain Fierro flew out over the Pacific, banked and opened a window so that Lowell might get a photo of Puerto Vallarta from on high. He informed us that on our return to Tepic we would be flying at an altitude of 6,000 ft. and our cruising speed would be 120-150 miles per hour. How's that? We could have made the trip by bus — the open-air jobs where you can get on at either side and the seats stretch across the bus. We heard of one woman who would not fly to Puerto Vallarta. She insisted on coming by bus but the memory of 12 hours of bouncing, crashing, soaring, and flying on her own impelled her to return to Tepic BY PLANE, however so small.

Captain Fierro's courtesy to Lowell allowed him to take a shot of Puerto Vallarta from the air. Part of the airplane wing shows in the foreground and in the center, ocean front, our Hotel El Paraíso.

Antigua, once the capital of Guatemala, presents remarkable architectural ruins, the result of the devastating earthquake of 1773. *Above,* the remains of a monastery. *Right,* all that is left of the magnificent Cathedral dedicated to San José. There was still carving to be seen in the niches.

A GAMBOL IN GUATEMALA AND ON TO YUCATAN

Mexico City: we took off in the rain — seats 2B and 2C, flight 501, Pan Am Clipper "Skylark," June 29, 1952 — en route to Yucatán. But Guatemala got in the way. When the plane stopped there, we decided we would also, an opportunity we didn't think we'd have again.

Down at Guatemala City and transfer to San Carlos Hotel, as an

Weaving seemed to be a cottage industry in one of the lakeshore villages. The girl is working with the ancient technique of the backstrap loom.

itinerary would say, if we had had one. I could make that arrival more flowery but I won't. I'll just say it was charming, the air was soft, and the music of marimbas floated through the hotel. Plenty of bars, too. There seemed to be three, unfortunately.

At dinner that night we ate a fruit called *pitahaya* — orange red, petal-like outside, purple with black seeds inside — sprinkled with sugar and lime juice. Delicious. We also had crab soup, guacamole, *chiles rellenos,* rice, beef, chayote, iced tea and pineapple. Carry me out.

Since we couldn't retire for the night on that we took a bus ride, five cents each, around the city. It is customary in Guatemala to thank the driver as you alight from the bus. We did, remembering an old saying . . . When in Rome, etc. We talked to some U.S. school teachers on that ride who said they had been in Guatemala two hours and hadn't heard a marimba. We told them not to worry, just hang in there.

Eggs, beans, rice, tortillas and *pan dulce* were excellent breakfast fare. Eggs could be "screembled" or "parched." Don't go into that sunny-side-up business unless your Spanish is better than ours.

Coffee was served at every meal, and who can forget that fragrant amber brew, Guatemalan coffee!

On a clear day, after a squab lunch, we stepped over to the Parque Central to take pictures of the flowers and fountain and nearly drowned the caretaker. The fountain was dry, so Lowell asked the man if he would turn on the water. He nodded graciously, lifted a large iron lid, disappeared down a hole, and BINGO! jets of water. The catch was, the hole was under the fountain. The caretaker received an extra quetzal.

Since we were in Guatemala a must was a trip to the highlands, and we made the grand tour from Antígua to Quetzaltenango with many stops coming and going. Sololá was fascinating. At Panajachel we ate zapotes — black, sweet and creamy. In Antigua at Posada

Lake Atitlán in the black and white version of the "Thunder Over Paradise picture," from the garden of Hotel Tzanjuyú.

Above, a girl was selling delectable pitahayas in another village on the lake shore. *Right,* a small part of the market in the central plaza of Santo Tomás Chichicastenango. Lowell used shallow depth of focus to emphasize right foreground figures.

Belém we were served black beans and fried bananas, divine! At Chichicastenango we took rooms at the Mayan Inn where barefoot boys in regional costume serve you. The Indian market there fills the entire plaza. Indians burned incense up the steps of Santo Tomás, a large church at one end of the market. Inside, rose petals covered the floor and many lighted candles scented the air. Bags, sashes, vegetables, sandals, pottery, and a hundred other regional artifacts gave the market a primitive charm. For 42 cents I bought a handful of earrings for my pierced ears. They looked just like Christmas tree balls and all the women were wearing them. Outside of the market Chichi had little to offer so we went on to Quetzaltenango. A quick look around, and we returned to Lake Atitlán with the three volcanoes above its shores: Atitlán, 11,565 ft.; San Pedro, 9,921 ft. and Toliman, 10,270 ft. I call Lowell's color photo of it "Thunder over Paradise." Each highland village had its own charm, distinct dress and customs, and each one was as impossible to forget as the vivid green mountains and precipitous gorges.

The day always comes when birds of passage have to move on, so back we went to Guatemala City to board the plane to Mérida. Lucky us, it was the Skylark again, and in 40 minutes we were in Yucatán, temperature 92, humidity same.

Taxi to Mayaland Lodge and Chichén Itzá. In this sun drenched limestone land we broiled. At breakfast each day we told our disgrun-

tled muscles to shape up as we needed their full cooperation if we were to see and climb the amazing ruins: El Castillo, the Temple of the Warriors, Temple of the Jaguars, El Caracol, the Tzompantli, a wall of carved skulls. The Sacred Well was haunting, and stories of the Great Ball Court rather gruesome. We crawled over them all and collapsed in our mosquito netting canopied beds at night. Chichén had a steady stream of visitors and we could understand its lure.

We were weary with all that hiking but weariness vanished when we were served such succulent dishes as *cochinita pibil* (pit-barbe-cued pork); flaky *empanadas* (turnovers) filled with vegetables; venison; beans; jellied fruit; broiled bananas, and spicy *panuchos* bursting with beans and shredded meat. The dining room at the lodge is open and a spider monkey joined us for dinner one evening, stealing sugar from the bowls on each table.

After dinner we would sit on a small terrace looking toward moon-lit El Caracol, and listen to soft guitars. The young men and girls who waited table danced in the patio, the girls with full bottles of wine balanced on their heads.

As usual, time ran out. We hied back to Mérida for the return to Mexico City and a more modern world. I can't believe it! My diary says we left for Acapulco the following morning. Say it isn't so. Dim the lights. I'll reminisce about that another day.

We visited this Maya home through the courtesy of our guide. The lady on the left was his friend and she let us "tour" her home. The family slept in hammocks, and cooking was done over coals on a dirt floor.

The Temple of Kukulkán or El Castillo, at Chichén Itzá, as it appears from
the Temple of the Warriors. A stairway rising in the center of the pyramid
leads to an inner temple where an impressive red-painted statue of a jaguar
with green stone incrustations is on view.

Our dear friend and driver Rafael Aldeco with "our" car, backdropped by snow-covered Iztaccihuatl, the Sleeping Lady who dreams on.

WE'RE OFF ON THE ROAD TO OAXACA

Here we go — or there we went — rolling down to Oaxaca in the "Blue Angel." That was Rafael's car. He was our friend and guide, and with him we had traveled Mexico north, east, and west. Now we were heading into the deep south, 330 miles from the capital. It was Thursday, November 11, 1954, 8:15 a.m. Rafael remarked the one thing that always had to be in blue ribbon condition on his car was the horn. That was a funny, but in those days he who blew loudest and first survived to blow again some other day. You will recall the noise, no doubt if you visited Mexico before the government banned blasts from that essential weapon, essential to the Mexican driver, that is.

If you are seeking a lazy siesta in the sun, Oaxaca is not your dish of frijoles. Too many interesting people, villages, foods, and ruins to stimulate your imagination and increase your blood sugar. For instance, a wayside bakery with a primitive brick kiln for an oven called for a halt. The bread looked, smelled, and tasted delicious. It was magenta color inside, brown and crusty outside, and this delight cost all of forty (40) centavos a loaf, three cents U.S. That and our box lunches and ice cold beer saw us through the day, and at 8:00 p.m., 11 hours and 45 minutes road time we stopped at the Marqués del Valle Hotel on the plaza.

Our room, 411, overlooking the plaza, cost a modest 90 pesos a day, $7.20 U.S., with meals, and for two. Below all was confusion. The hotel and Avenida Hidalgo swarmed with racing drivers, their cars, and mechanics, not to mention the curious young *indios,* awed and thrilled by the excitement. The last Great Mexican Road Race from Tuxtla Gutiérrez to the U.S. border at El Paso, Texas, was to begin November 19th, and this city was one gathering point.

We ate a typical Oaxaca dinner that night: ranchero soup, tamales Oaxaca style wrapped in banana leaves, pork *mole,* hot chiles, tortillas, and hot chocolate. We could scarcely wait to begin and could scarcely get up when we finished. Happily stuffed we went to bed and listened to the music of the marimbas coming from under the laurel trees across the plaza. We popped up early the next morning, anticipating the day and ready for *huevos rancheros,* served with firecrackers as I remember.

Oaxaca, in its cool mountain valley, has a pleasant climate. The avenues are shaded by magnificent trees and lined with colonial style buildings, many with carved facades of pale green stone. We visited the Cathedral, Santo Domingo and La Soledad churches, handsome, ornate, majestic. There seemed to be no nightlife but a poster in the lobby of our hotel directed us to the Hotel Monte Albán to see *La Danza de La Pluma,* the Feather Dance. The per-

Rafael and his *gringa* friend anxiously waiting for a loaf of bread from this primitive wayside oven. Neither one of us needed it if you are observing the rear views.

formers wore multicolored ribboned costumes with headdresses fashioned of brilliantly colored feathers and flashing mirrors. It was all so dazzling we were glad to give our eyes a rest as we emerged into a gentle rain.

Saturday was market day, with vendors from all the surrounding villages in attendance, and we wandered through a tangle of hundreds of stalls filled with flowers, fruits, cheeses, sarapes, vegetables, gold filigree jewelry, and animals (domestic).

Just a short distance from the city of Oaxaca is the village of San Bartolo Coyotepec where we found the home of Doña Rosa. You've heard of her, I know. This small Oaxaqueña was famous for her prized black pottery. Museums throughout the world display her artistry.

A daily ritual began about 4:00 each afternoon. We sat under the portales in front of our hotel drinking beer and *ponche* and exchanging lies with other visiting firemen. But it was early to bed because the days were always full.

Today, Monte Albán! Visible from the city, and seven miles southwest lie the archaeological remains of this sacred capital of the Zapotecs. Treasures removed from the tombs are to be seen in

Doña Rosa of Coyotepec, master potter and gracious lady. Lowell set up his Speed Graphic with delayed action to get himself taking a picture of Rosa.

Doña Rosa in action. Her husband Juventino burnished all the pots she made with a small pottery shard.

the museum in town; don't miss them. One of the richest finds came from Tomb 7, a fabulous cache of gold masks, jewelry, pearls, jade, amber, rock crystal, and alabaster bowls. We perspired (make that, sweated) over the 15 square miles that encompass pyramids, sunken courts, immense stairways (one 135 feet wide), a ball court, and a number of curious human figures carved on huge stone slabs.

Next day we set off to conquer Mitla, 25 miles southeast of Oaxaca. The dewy, soft early morning air seemed to have called everyone, including dogs and burros, out on the road. We passed one small lad who was selling candy from a board balanced on his head. "How about some dysentery?" inquired Mr. Weeks. I declined. One does not repeat an indiscretion of that nature.

As we slowly walked through this timeworn ruin our guide informed us that the scorching sun had preserved the buildings with their stone fretwork almost as they were centuries before. Luckily, the site is much smaller than Monte Albán, and we didn't linger. I had no hat, and the scorching sun was preserving by head. Isn't it odd, or is it? how you punish yourself so you won't miss a thing

Looking out over two thousand years of history and wondering what went on here when Monte Albán was a great ceremonial center and not the ruin it is today.

and come home to have someone say, "Oh, too bad you missed it!" Nuts!

Shade in the car was welcome, and so was the coolness under the largest tree in Mexico, at nearby Santa María del Tule. It is 165 feet high with a circumference of 160 feet. It's supposed to have sheltered Hernán Cortés. Someone told me this. I hope it is true. I make an effort to be correct in these remembrances, along with my daily diary, but if I don't make a mistake, that will be the day.

Eventually we rolled on south, to tropical Tehuantepec on the river of the same name. Hot, buggy and humid. Our room at Hotel Tehuantepec was 35 pesos, $2.50 U.S., double, if you care to know how life used to be BI and BTMT (Before Inflation and Before Too Many Tourists). In this climate fruits attain perfection — banana, papaya, mango, guava, pomegranate, star apple, custard apple, and so on and on. It was from Hotel Tehuantepec that we saw the first lap of the Great Road Race.

Beauty and brains are one on the Isthmus. The *tehuana* is admired for her regal bearing and business acumen. She does the market trading and her husband works in the fields or stays at home. The choice of color and style of her dress would make a couturier envious: a bolero type blouse of embroidered cotton, next a bare midriff, then a long skirt of brilliant cloth with white lace flounce, set off by cinnamon skin, black eyes, and luxuriant black braids twined with colorful ribbons. How I admired these beauties for I am short and freckled.

The market place over which the women preside is a mélange of fruits and vegetables. On one visit we watched, wide-eyed, as a *tehuana* submerged a bare arm in a washtub of orange juice and stirred vigorously. We noted the live armadillos tethered about. Deshelled and stewed they are very tasty. (I know this only from hearsay.) There were also thousands of varicolored beads, caged birds looking like feathered jewels, handicrafts, sacks of seed, and clothing, including the *resplandor,* an elaborate headdress made in the shape of a long-armed baby dress. I know, I bought one, and I was not a success wearing it. Gold was displayed here and there. Twenty-four carat coins from a U.S. mint, heirlooms "inherited" from U.S. engineers who were here in the last half of the 19th century

This scene, taken in Etla, reminds me of biblical times. Not that I lived then but it evokes that feeling — the ancient cart, the patient oxen, and the angelic little man.

Left, the *resplandor,* a fantastic white lace headdress peculiar to the Tehuantepec area, is worn on festive occasions. *Below,* in the matriarchal society of Juchitán you see no men at the daily market. It was here we watched bug-eyed as a matron plunged her arm into a wash tub full of orange juice, and stirred vigorously.

Juliana, she of the "all married men stink like bedbugs" comment.

working on a railroad across the isthmus. At that time a Panama-type canal was a consideration.

We found a truly snooty beauty down the road a piece in the town of Juchitán. While graciously posing for pictures she mentioned women in this region are known as *shuncas*, then added this startling tidbit — all married men stink like bedbugs. Wild!! Lowell photographed a wedding proccesion that day, too. The bride was in white with flowing veil. The men well groomed in black suits, while proud mama teetered along in high heels, almost illuminated in electric blue satin and sweat.

My place in the car was the middle seat between Rafael and Lowell. One day at lunch I ordered some delectable dish which came with a plentiful supply of chopped fresh onion. Both men joined the raised eyebrow department as they eyed my choice. When we left the café, Rafael turned to me, "Señora Dorothy, when we are in the car, speak me sideways, please."

Back in Oaxaca we stopped for another look at battle scarred Santo Domingo, several times vandalized and plundered but now restored. The ceiling of the chapel must be the most unusual in Mexico; it is the genealogical tree of the Virgin. The branches are covered with saints' heads, bunches of grapes, chubby cherubs, angels, and what-not, all in high relief and all splashed with gold.

Somehow, each place we visited overshadowed the one before. Along the ancient routes of Mexico we found new vistas, experiences. Adventures were always waiting just around the bend in the road.

The inset from the tiled bench opposite shows the vanilla orchid vine with its lovely white blossoms which last only a day or two.

VANILLA VIGNETTE

That vanilla was a flavoring was all we knew about it when we poked our noses into the land of tamales and tequila in June 1958. And suddenly there we were in the moist tropics with white-clad Totonac Indians and a rain forest where the trees are duennas to the clinging vines of the vanilla orchid. We arrived in Papantla, state of Veracruz, via Pachuca, Tulancingo, and Poza Rica. Actually, we were on our way to the port of Veracruz but who, unless afflicted with anosmia, could drive right through an area where the air was delicious with the scent of vanilla. No argument there.

When Hernán Cortés began his conquest of Mexico in 1519, one of the secrets he acquired from the ill-starred Indians with their gleaming white cities, temples atop pyramids, and mountains of gold and silver, was their unrivaled knowledge of vanilla. *Xanath* (shanath) they called it, and their favorite beverage was made of chocolate and vanilla beans, both roasted, ground, mixed with water and whipped to a feathery foam. At Cortés' orders, cuttings of the singular vine orchid were sent to Spain.

Papantla is the vanilla capital of the world and the Totonacs, who cultivate the vines, are perhaps Mexico's most prosperous Indian group. Headquarters for the growing and distribution of the sweet smelling harvest of this member of the orchid family (*Vanilla planifolia*) are the villages of Papantla and Gutiérrez Zamora. In the surrounding rain forest, where the vanilla orchid first grew wild, the Totonacs hand-pollinate the waxy white flowers when they appear in early spring. After pollination the beans grow slowly during the moist tropical summer, sheltered and shaded from the jungle sun. In November the pods are gathered and the curing process begins.

After a three-day roasting period the beans are given a steam bath. Then comes the sun-curing cycle. Each morning, thousands of ripening pods are carefully placed in the sun. At noon each day, they are carried inside the compound to rest on special racks which allow air to circulate freely. The next morning they are again placed in the sun and so on, a daily ritual. This alternate drying and sweating reduces the moisture content and intensifies the aromatic granules within the pod. After six months of this tender care the deep brown beans, mellowed by time and sun, are sorted and bound in packets, ready for market. It is during this phase in the career of the beans that the aroma of vanilla perfumes the *ambiente* with a heady fragrance for miles around. Some are used for extract, some for liqueurs, and some reach their destination as luscious, sticky whole beans.

Inspired by personal contact with the Midas vine of the Indians, we learned how to use the whole bean as they do. But since the extract is made by distillation we had to experiment with a less complicated process and came up with an infusion of Southern Comfort and the ripe bean. As a result, we present a bold claim to possessing the most impudent vanilla north of the border. When our bottle gets low, more (S.C.) is added, more beans poked in, and the fertile union continues. My bottle has more than 23 years.

If you cannot go to Papantla for beans (or can you?) look around your market or specialty store and you will find them,

Lowell purposely photographed this ornate tiled bench in Papantla's main plaza for the center inset of a Totonac girl and vanilla vine.

These young men were as perfumed as the product. As they went by us in the vanilla bean sorting room we could have swooned with the fragrance.

usually in a small glass vial. Rejoice! Now, buy a bottle of Southern Comfort, one-pint size, pour out some (you might drink this, adding to the occasion), put in the beans which you have cut into two-inch lengths, cap the bottle tightly, and wait for your reward. Why did I choose S.C.? I thought it would be a smoother, tastier base. As a lagniappe I'll add here that I keep a squat jar filled with sugar in which I place cut beans and whole nutmegs. Thus I enrich my desserts.

Now that you have the flavor of this sortie, we have a feeling you'll be more impressed with your culinary efforts crowned with *V. planifolia* and remember, as we do, that this universal flavoring is a rapturous blend of rain forest, jungle sun, the labor of white-clad Totonac Indians, and emerald green vines laden with orchids.

This little bride and groom in Papantla were very hesitant to pose for a picture until they understood it was free. A copy of this photo was sent to them, care of the village *Jefe*. I hope they received it.

WE CHOOSE VERACRUZ

Saturated with vanilla we drove on to the city of Veracruz, the long way, inland through Jalapa ablaze with myriad flowers. Our arrival at Veracruz was tempestuous. In 1519 the Spaniards sailed in on a storm of conquest. In 1958 we blew in to Veracruz on a storm of nature. Blinding rain had plagued us for many miles before we reached the port on the Gulf of Mexico. Then, in our room at the Hotel Emporio on the boardwalk, a tropical storm, squally and blustering, lifted the rug off the floor and meant to have it too, as it screamed and whistled beneath the French doors facing the bay. Rain came in through the window casements. In spite of the violence and our fatigue, we dressed and went to dinner. I've no idea what we ate. I didn't write in my diary that night. We just hoped the hotel was anchored to windward and tumbled into bed.

Surprise! We awoke to a glorious morning, sunbeams everywhere. That's a typical Veracruz weather report. Tempest yesterday; tran-

One of the delights of Veracruz is the distinctive music, and we were fortunate to meet this group of sidewalk musicians.

quility today. Discomfort forgotten and breakfast over, we bustled out, Lowell with cameras, I with map, brochure and diary. Across the way, the ancient fortress of San Juan de Ulúa showed its ugly face. Guidebook said visit, so we did. It was revolting, grim, dark and dank, with a grisly history of gory murders, devilish cruelty, greed, and horrifying dungeons. Lowell didn't shoot one piece of film. So much for número uno.

Back on the avenida we bumped into a strolling trio ready to play *arpa, vihuela,* and *jarana* (a harp and two types of guitar). A small boy with the group danced a *zapateado* for us; total cost, 20 pesos. The market was close by. Markets, as you know by now, act on me like magnets. And the Veracruz market was dazzling, fruits, flowers and fish! I never saw so many fish — all shapes, sizes, and colors. No bartering here. Pay the price asked. I wondered what the fish were but, even if I had been told, I wouldn't have remembered the Spanish names. I recognized only the clumsy turtles moping around the cement floor.

Fresh oysters anyone? The small fishing village of Mandinga lured us ten miles south. In a very informal, open-air thatched roof shack we were served oysters, crab and shrimp, so fresh they practically jumped from the lagoon onto our plates. A North American seated nearby pointed to a pile of shells on his table and said he had just consumed 48 oysters, a plate each of crab and shrimp, washed down with beer AND rum. Then added his home was in Veracruz, minutes away, but he NEVER ate fish there. By the time it reached the city it was stale! Crazy! Our feast for three, Lowell, Rafael and me, was $1.52 U.S. I could cry in my beer thinking about it now. Forty-eight oysters at my market today would cost $19.20. Pearls at any price, though. That's my opinion.

Heaven forbid that we go to Veracruz and not eat *huachinango a la veracruzana* (red snapper Veracruz style). Therefore, we purposely tried a variety of restaurants, always ordering that famous dish. Each had an excellent version and one restaurant also served superb black beans as well as *caldo largo de camarones* (shrimp broth).

After we admired the old homes with their carved wooden balconies, and walked around the wharves inhaling the fragrance of coffee, vanilla, and molasses, we decided the best pictures were from the sidewalk cafés and open-air streetcars. The city was very untouristy and that we liked. We feel fortunate to have experienced Mexico's undemanding pace of years ago. If my remembrances read as though we ate and drank our way around, guess we did. We were young and, as Mr. Thoreau said, "Time is but the stream we go fishing in." Must say we have caught our share.

Where we ate at Mandinga — the small thatched shelter in the center of the photo.

The Plaza Grande in colonial Pátzcuaro which on market days was crowded with people, produce, and craft articles.

PATZCUARO REVISITED - 1956

The simple act of buying two Pullman tickets to Pátzcuaro led to the night we declared war on the railroad system of Mexico. We think conductors should ring bells, blow the whistle, shout the Spanish equivalent of "ALL ABOARRRD," and not fold up their tents like the Arabs and silently steal away.

We had anticipated leaving Mexico City on schedule at 9:30 p.m. but, by some whim or caprice, our train was still sulking under the shed at 10:30. From behind the curtains of my berth I heard my husband, in quiet desperation, ask the porter when we would leave. He replied, "in 20 minutes." Lowell skipped off the train, sprinted into the station rest-room, zoomed out . . . and sagged. No train, Just like those Arabs, we had vanished. He says he clapped hand to brow in pure East Lynn anguish, while on the train I increased my blood pressure by 1,000 points.

With singleness of purpose I tried to dress (I sleep nude) in the bedlam of my berth. Everything seemed to elude me in the confusion of clothes, maps, slippers, blankets, hairpins, Kleenex, travel folders. In and out, bawling and blowing, scrambling and hunting, pushing the button for the porter and screaming, "Stop the train! Lemme off! Kill the engineer! Oh, my poor husband! Throw off our luggage! Send up flares! Call Washington!

That shows you how inconsistent one can be in moments of stress. What a waste of powder and shout! The porter counterblasted with, "Primera, primera" (First, first) while I continued to rip and roar. Twenty minutes later we "primera-ed" at the first station down the line, and who staggered down the aisle, receiving fuertes *abrazos* from the porter and the conductor? My husband!

How did Lowell make the train? A knowledgeable taxi driver, noting his predicament, scooped him up, charged off into the night and delivered him at the first stop. With us and the train underway, we tried to settle down, noting the sign posted at the end of our coach:

QUIETUD PARA EL BENEFICIO DE LOS QUE DESCANSAN
(Quiet for the benefit of those who are resting)

Despite our willingness to comply with the admonition we spent a restless night in horizontal versions of St. Vitus' dance. When morning finally came we looked out at the beautiful purple hills of Michoacán. In the fields, natives were picking strawberries, and wraith-like vapors floated above the tules. The scene was so tranquil and serene that we smoked the peace pipe with our overstimulated nerves and bolstered our sabotaged strength with a breakfast of potato chips, candied *camotes* (sweet potatoes), and Orange Crush, an unlikely combination but the only food available on our iron horse.

Tardy by two and one-half hours, we arrived in Pátzcuaro, a centuries-old village replete with legends and mystery, Indian culture and tradition, quaint customs and dances, an immense lake and the butterfly fishermen. Towering ash trees shade the age worn buildings and cobblestone streets of this rural community 250 miles west of Mexico City. One hubbub it shares with the Mexican countryside everywhere is morning noise — dogs, roosters, burros, and church bells. The Tarascan Indians of the region are much in evidence, proud, arrogant and, as such, completely provincial; they cling to their old ways, totally indifferent to change.

Gloating over our good fortune to be there again we rented lodgings at the Posada de la Basilica and "yielded ourselves up to the charm of Pátzcuaro and environs," as the travel book suggested.

We rediscovered the Plaza Chica and the Plaza Grande and found they hadn't changed in eight years. We drove up to El Estribo and gazed out over the lake to see if the statue of Morelos still stood watch over the island of Janitzio. Yes, he was there. We inched along in the usual people jam of the Friday market and bought flamboyant flowers, woolen rebozos, the locally made pottery with fish designs in black on a cream background, and masks: terrifying, ridiculous, magnificent.

We ate the delicate flavored *pescado blanco* (whitefish) fresh from the lake, fried, wrapped in tortilla, and fiery with *salsa picante*. We lingered in the museum, built in 1540 to house San Nicolás College, where the past still cast its shadow — barely excavated pre-Hispanic ruins filled the garden. We daydreamed in the atrium of the Basilica, its adobe walls clothed in moss.

We visited the rambling 18th-century Convento de las Catarinas (I have been told that it has since been restored and transformed into an artisan center and renamed the "House of the Eleven Patios;" dilapidated as it was when we explored it, there were at least 11 countable) and the adjacent church, El Sagrario. There, a Tarascan acquaintance told us this tale of the construction of convent and church:

"Long, long ago, the good Padre wanted to build a church and convent because the people needed them. He had many disap-

Everyday scene, master, dog, and burros with panniers of charcoal.

islands in the lake, but the most interesting to us. These fishermen were ready to pose, one peso per man, then!

pointments trying to collect the money and construction went so slowly that, desperate, he prayed to the Virgin, very deeply, and one night she sent a crew of angels. When morning came, the Padre woke to find the church and convent finished, and much more beautiful than he had dreamed. Nor was that all. A special gift from the angels was the church ceiling, painted midnight blue with stars of silver."

Restoration was beginning when we were there but the workers we saw were of a more earthy type.

Fear of missing something stabbed us with an energy that rivaled Stephen Leacock's character "who got on his horse and rode off in all directions." One day we drove in the rain to Erongarícuaro, past marsh tules, a Spanish castle on an island, whipped cream clouds in a stormy sky, pink ginger flowers, and mud, to buy the handsome cotton textiles woven there.

We hastened to another lake village Tzintzuntzan (Place of the Hummingbirds) where we were able to purchase exquisite feather-

Usually when photographed, the "butterfly" nets are wrapped as shown in the foreground. However, the two fishermen behind obliged Lowell by showing the procedure used when fishing for *charalitos*.

work. We climbed to the Tarascan ruins on the eastern edge of the village and investigated the *yacatas,* five keyhole shaped structures that stand on a several leveled base. Once a capital of the Tarascan Empire (Pátzcuaro was the other center), the Spaniards built a huge Franciscan monastery in Tzintzuntzan for the prompt conversion of the area's inhabitants. The atrium was filled with olive trees planted by the first friars 450 years ago. Somewhat wizened they were, but still bearing fruit.

A short drive south put us under the thatched roof of a patio in the town of Santa Clara del Cobre where we watched in admiration as glowing blobs of copper were tempered and hammered into a variety of shapes from platters to pots.

The region's colorful native dances are not to be ignored, so back to the Posada de Don Vasco, where we had stayed on our previous trip, to see again *Los Viejitos* (The Little Old Men). Again we laughed at the antics and applauded the youths who, pretending to be old men complete with long white locks and masks portraying aged faces, began the dance hobbling about on sturdy canes. Then, inspired by the gay strains of a native guitar, their movements became more agile until, suddenly, they struck the floor three times with their canes and their nimbleness was astounding. The dance ended on a return to sedate senility.

Near the Posada de Don Vasco, we invited ourselves in to a lovely walled mansion to investigate the CREFAL (meaning, in English, Center for Fundamental Education in Latin America), a UNESCO organization dedicated to training teachers from all over Latin America in subjects and techniques basic to improving living standards in rural areas.

As often as we could, we wrenched ourselves away from the mainland long enough to fall in love with the islands once more. Big launch, little launch, dugout canoe, we traveled around and about the lake in all of them to visit even the smallest nub of solid ground. But our favorite was Janitzio, the home of the "butterfly fishermen." They don't fish for butterflies; the nets they use resemble butterfly wings, hence the name. Our guess was that they are the most photographed fishermen in the world; they posed readily for a one-peso-per-man fee. On this island stands the 135-foot high statue of José María Morelos y Pavón, patriot of the War for Independence, one defiant arm raised. We were able to scrape up enough fortitude to make the climb to the uplifted hand. When we reached the top, after struggling up the corkscrew stairway past seemingly miles of murals depicting the life of Morelos, we were

We stopped for "lunch" here in Janitzio, on returning from a visit to the Morelos statue atop the island. The tiny fish (charalitos) fresh from the lake, hot chile sauce, tortillas, and cold beer made a never-to-be-forgotten memory. Note lake in the background through the cook's "window."

Fish nets drying on Janitzio. To make this a competition quality print, Lowell eliminated seven people from the photo: one sitting by the woman, five to her right, and one to the left of the man in the dugout. By cutting, inserting and pasting, this picture, enlarged to 14" x 20," won blue ribbons in salons worldwide.

breathless. There, the condition was intensified — the view was breathtaking, too.

We shopped every day, what else? Everything was offered: textiles, pottery, rebozos, wood carving, silver jewelry and lacquerware. From the display of clay *santos,* we brought La Virgen de la Salud home to preside over our patio. The laquerware made in Pátzcuaro is outstanding. When we were there, such fame had the reigning master, Salvador Solchaga, that his exquisite trays with their tastefully colored designs traced in gold had been purchased for display by museums in the United States and Europe.

In my memory linger some tales of Pátzcuaro. For instance, legend has it that centuries ago Caltzontzin, the last king to rule the mighty Tarascan empire, watched the waters of the lake close over his priceless treasures in order to save them from the avid hands of the Spaniards. Do the fish and watersnakes still guard the treasure today? ¿Quién sabe? And who knows what phantoms might appear if you pay a late night visit to the lake. 'Tis said that if you put your ear to the surface at exactly twelve o'clock midnight you will hear the golden bells ring.

And another tale of poignant charm told to me by a member of a family prominent in Pátzcuaro for many generations: "Why are there water lilies in the lake? Well, once long ago there was a warrior. He had to leave but he told his sweetheart to go to the lake on moonlit nights and there she would see his face in the water. Time after time she saw him, but one night his image did not appear. She walked into the lake, searching for him, and drowned. From her come the water lilies, and when droplets form on the lilies they are not dew but her tears." Makes me cry, also.

Came a day when we had to make a decision and, hesitating between a "balk and a breakdown" (we borrowed that from Uncle Remus), we decided to chance the return trip to Mexico City by rail — I can report only a prompt departure and a very dull ride. After all, my travel folder said, "Go Pullman, Pátzcuaro is connected with Mexico City by rail." How well we know!

END OF MEMORIES, ON TO RECIPES

APPETIZERS

Tostadas de calabacitas (zucchini tostadas)

6 flour tortillas   4 small, fresh zucchini, shredded
1 medium onion, finely chopped   6 Tbsp. Jack cheese, shredded
jalapeño chile(s), fresh or canned, chopped (amount depends on your
   endurance)

Fry flour tortillas quickly in hot fat on both sides. They should be crisp. Top with shredded fresh zucchini and chopped green chile. Sprinkle with finely chopped onion and shredded Jack cheese. Serve with ice cold beer and the following *sauce*:

In blender put two peeled ripe tomatoes, one sweet red pepper and one green. Salt to taste. If you wish the salsa hot, add dashes of Tabasco sauce to taste.

Mexican Potato Chips

Sprinkle large potato chips with grated Jack cheese and minced jalapeño chile. Broil to melt cheese. Serve immediately.

Anchovy Tostadas

Spread crisp fried flour tortillas with anchovies mashed with olive oil to make a paste. Top with guacamole and a light sprinkle of chile powder.

Quesadillas

8 flour tortillas   one 7 oz. can green chiles, cut into 16 strips
8 sprigs cilantro   8 slices Monterey Jack cheese

Heat iron skillet or griddle and warm tortillas, turning them until soft and pliable. Place strips of cheese, one sprig cilantro, and two strips chile on each tortilla and fold in half. Place in oven until tortillas are hot and cheese is melted. Serve hot.

Jalisco Dip

3 cloves garlic   2 Tbsp. lime juice
1/4 tsp. salt   1 cup mushrooms, minced
1 cube butter   1 carton (7-8 oz.) Jalisco Jocoque
1 tsp. onion, grated   (now in markets in my area; one
1 tsp. anchovy paste   cup sour cream may be substi-
                           tuted)

Mash garlic cloves to a pulp, with the salt. Melt one cube butter, add garlic, grated onion, lime juice, and minced mushrooms. Sauté for four minutes Remove from heat and add the *jocoque* (a thick buttermilk), or sour cream. Beat thoroughly and serve with vegetable strips and warm tortillas.

Sopa de Queso (Cheese Soup)

1 white onion	1 quart milk
1 green onion	3 cups water
1 medium tomato, skinned	3 cups Cheddar cheese, cubed
2 poblano chiles	4 medium potatoes, peeled and
1 Tbsp. oil	coarsely chopped

Fry coarsely chopped potatoes, sliced onions, chopped tomato, and chiles previously roasted, peeled and cut into strips (see section on "Chiles" for preparation). Then add milk and salt. When milk begins to simmer, add water and allow to *simmer* until potatoes are cooked. Add cheese just before serving. Cover to allow cheese to melt slightly. *Note:* You may substitute canned green chiles instead of poblano chiles, to cut down on preparation time.

Bean Soup a la Naranja

2 cups black bean soup	3 Tbsp. Curaçao or other orange
fresh orange segments	liqueur

You can find black bean soup in cans although I usually make it from scratch — cook the beans and then blend with sufficient bean broth to the proper consistency — it should be very smooth. Heat bean soup, add Curaçao. Pour into bowls, add orange segments and serve immediately. The above quantities are sufficient for two servings, but may be increased at will.

Onion-Parsley Soup

1 lb. small white onions	2 cups water
2 Tbsp. parsley	3 cups chicken broth
1 Tbsp. oregano	1 Tbsp. bottled jalapeño chile sauce
½ cup Monterrey cheese, shredded	salt to taste

Put onions in water, bring to boil and simmer about 20 minutes. Then put in blender with the parsley, and purée. Add mixture to the chicken broth with the oregano, jalapeño sauce, and salt if necessary. Heat to serve, and sprinkle with the cheese.

Instead of topping with the cheese, a swirl of sour cream with ¼ tsp. lime juice on top is also very good.

Cilantro-Parsley Soup

4 cups chicken broth	½ cup cilantro, chopped
1 cup parsley, chopped	1 green onion, minced
2 Tbsp. butter	salt and pepper

Melt butter in pan, add cilantro, parsley and green onion. Cook five minutes. Have broth boiling, stir into cilantro mixture, add salt and pepper to taste. Serve with Mexican garlic bread (See "Fillers").

Sopa de Lentejas (Lentil Soup)

1½ cups lentils, brown if possible
½ cup tomato, chopped
¼ cup seeded canned green chile, diced
½ lb. chorizo, cut in chunks
parsley sprigs
½ cup onion, minced
1 medium clove garlic
¼ tsp. cumin
2 Tbsp. oil
croutons
Mexican cheese (crumbly white)

Wash and soak lentils in cold water for two hours. Drain. Brown chorizo in oil. Add lentils along with onion, tomato, garlic, chile and cumin. Add three quarts of boiling water. Cover and simmer two hours. Serve with croutons, which have been browned in garlic oil, parsley sprigs, and a sprinkling of cheese.

Crab bisque a la mexicana

1 lb. crab meat, fresh or thawed
4 Tbsp. flour
½ tsp. salt
2 Tbsp. butter
4 cups milk, scalded
pinch white pepper

Melt butter, add flour, mix well, add hot milk slowly. Stir constantly and cook over low heat until smooth. Add crab meat. Keep hot while making the *sauce:*

1 small can tomatillos
1 Tbsp. oil
½ tsp. cumin
salt to taste
½ chile jalapeño, chopped
1 very small clove garlic or pinch of garlic powder

Blend all ingredients until smooth.

Pour hot bisque into bowls, float sauce over top. Serve with warm corn tortillas, jicama sticks (see "Vegetables"), and ice cold beer. Delicious? You said a spoonful.

Tortilla Soup(s)

Following are two versions of this excellent soup; the most usual first:

6 day-old corn tortillas, cut into strips about ½ inch wide
cooking oil, sufficient to fry tortilla strips.
4 cups chicken broth, preferably homemade but canned will do
1 pasilla chile, seeded
¼ medium onion
2 sprigs epazote
1 medium tomato, skinned
2 cloves garlic
½ cup Mexican white cheese, crumbled

Fry tortilla strips until golden brown. Parch (five seconds on each side on a hot griddle) pasilla chile. Blend tomato, onion and garlic until smooth. In 1½ Tbsp. of oil left from frying tortillas, fry tomato mixture for five minutes. Add chicken broth, chile pasilla, and epazote, and allow to simmer for ten minutes. Just before serving, add tortilla strips and barely bring to a boil. Serve immediately. Have cheese in a side dish to add, as desired.

The second version is one often served in Pátzcuaro:

6 day-old corn tortillas, cut into strips as above
cooking oil, sufficient to fry tortilla strips.
2 poblano chiles, peeled (See "Chiles") or 2 canned, green chiles, cut into narrow strips

4 cups chicken broth, as above	2 large tomatoes, skinned
¼ medium onion	2 cloves garlic
¾ cup thick cream	4 strips Mexican white cheese

Fry tortillas (as above). Prepare poblano chiles and cut into strips. Blend tomatoes, onion and garlic until smooth. Fry in $1^{1}/_{2}$ Tbsp. of oil for five minutes. Add chicken broth and simmer for 10 minutes. Just before serving, add cream and tortilla strips and heat to simmering. Serve immediately. Garnish each bowl with strips of chile and cheese.

FILLERS   (Rice and such)

Rice(s)

Mexican rice is fried before the liquid is added, not just boiled, Oriental style. Making good rice is as easy or difficult as making good pie crust or tenderly cooking eggs — it's simple once you know the tricks. The following recipes call for natural, white rice.

Basic proportions are one cup of rice to 2½ cups of liquid. First, soak the grains for ten minutes in scalding hot (not boiling) water; then rinse thoroughly in cold water. Drain and toss as dry as possible. Heat one-third cup vegetable oil (seems a lot but it isn't) and add rice. Stir occasionally so that each grain is coated evenly. When each grain is floating free in the oil, and they all *begin* to brown, drain off all oil possible (may be saved and reused) and add the liquid (see below) immediately to stop the frying process. This, of course, means that you should have the liquid ready before you start frying the rice. Avoid stirring the rice, except at the beginning of the cooking process — just after adding liquid and any tidbits to be used. Cook covered over moderate heat about 20 minutes or until liquid has been absorbed. If you wish to reheat you may either leave a small amount of liquid in the pot or add more of the same, or plain water at the time of reheating.

White Rice: In your blender, put the 2½ cups of water, one-quarter of a medium onion and several garlic cloves, 1½ tsp. salt or two chicken broth cubes: blend until smooth. This is your liquid; proceed as above.

Following are some of the more common varieties of rice depending upon the liquid used, and the occasional addition of tidbits. Once you have mastered the basic rice recipe (white), you are limited only by your imagination.

Red Rice: This is the traditional *arroz a la mexicana.*

Into your blender, put the 2½ cups water, one medium tomato, skinned, one-quarter of a medium onion, several garlic cloves, 1½ tsp. salt or two chicken broth cubes; blend until smooth. Proceed as above. Fresh carrots, chopped into small pieces, and fresh peas are usually added right after the liquid. If cooked or canned vegetables are used, add at end of cooking period, just giving them time to heat through.

Green Rice: Again follow basic recipe, but change taste and color of liquid by boiling it a few minutes with two husked tomatillos. Cool liquid, leaving in tomatillos, and blend with a goodly amount of parsley and one poblano chile. Strain liquid through coarse strainer before adding to rice.

Brown Rice: Made by using a very light, strained bean broth, preferably from black beans, as your liquid.

Once you've mastered the basic technique and each grain comes out plump and separate, try variations: add fresh mushrooms and raw chicken livers to white rice together with the liquid, or garnish with fried bananas. To the red, add zuchini and tiny green onions. To the green, strips of green pepper and garnish with pimiento. To the brown, small chunks of yellow crooked-neck squash and fresh corn cut from the cob, etc., etc.

Then there are the sauces that can accompany rice and make it still more versatile: guacamole; fresh or dried chile sauces; canned yellow or green chiles in vinaigrette.

And, if you wish to prepare an approximate version of Mexican rice without oil, here's how:

Spread one cup dry white rice in a shallow pan. Place in 400° oven and bake. Stir occasionally until golden brown. This rice may be stored, after baking, in a tightly capped glass jar, ready for immediate use. Continue as in rice recipes above, adding liquid and seasonings.

Jalapeño Corn Pudding

One and one-half 17 oz. cans creamed corn	1 cup (two sticks) butter, melted
1 cup corn meal	2 eggs, beaten
2 medium onions, chopped	2 cups Cheddar cheese, grated
½ tsp. soda	3 jalapeño chiles (fresh or canned), chopped
¾ cup buttermilk	

Mix everything but cheese and jalapeño chiles together. Place half of batter in greased baking dish. Cover with 1½ cups cheese and the chiles. Top with remaining batter and sprinkle on remaining half cup of cheese. Bake one hour at 350°.

Polenta Mexicana

1 cup corn meal
3 cups chicken broth
2 cups sharp cheese, grated
½ tsp. cumin

1 cup cold water
¼ lb. butter
1 small serrano chile, minced
salt to taste

Mix corn meal and cold water in heavy kettle. Bring chicken broth to a boil; stir into corn meal mixture with cumin, chile, butter and salt. Cook slowly until thick. Stir constantly until mixture goes "plop." Add cheese and stir until melted. Keep warm until serving time, and then mound on plates like mashed potatoes.

Green Corn Tamales

6 ears fresh corn in husks
1 tsp. salt
1½ cups white corn meal
strips of canned green chiles to taste

1-½ Tbsp. lard, softened (or Crisco)
1 Tbsp. sugar
6 strips sharp Cheddar cheese

Shuck corn, reserve husks. Cut kernels from cobs and whip in blender. Should have 1½ cups. Add salt and softened lard and enough corn meal to make a dough of spreading consistency. Flatten husks and spread with a layer of dough about ¼ inch thick. Cut cheese and chiles into strips and place on dough. Fold husks around filling and steam 40 minutes. Makes 8-12 tamales.

Mexican Garlic Bread

1 loaf French bread (baguette)
1 stick butter, softened
½ cup fresh cilantro, chopped

2 large cloves garlic, mashed
1 Tbsp. onion, grated

Slice loaf in half lengthwise. Spread with mixture of butter, mashed garlic, grated onion, and chopped cilantro. Press firmly together and wrap in damp towel. Refrigerate overnight. To serve, wrap in piece of greased foil and bake 25-30 minutes at 300°.

CHILES

Take small hot chiles — serranos, jalapeños, cascabeles, güeros — those that scorch your throat and lift the top off your head. Wash. Half fill glass jar with dry sherry, or sweet, or half and half. Add chiles until jar is full. Add more sherry to cover. For extra flavor, add any or all of the following: fresh thyme, fresh marjoram, bay leaves, whole garlic heads. Cap tightly and refrigerate. Keeps indefinitely.

Both liquid and chiles come in handy in many recipes. You may also cut some chiles in pieces as a garnish for soup, or serve them as appetizers. Warn your guests.

Chile Salad Vinaigrette

2 cups fresh jalapeño chiles, cut into quarters lengthwise, stems and seeds removed
1 cup fresh peas
10 whole garlic heads
8 carrots, cut into sticks
½ cup oil
1 cup water

2 cups small, whole fresh mushrooms
1 small cauliflower, in flowerettes
20 whole small onions
1 cup apple cider vinegar
4 bay leaves
sprigs of fresh thyme and marjoram

Fry chiles and all vegetables, except mushrooms, for two minutes. Add vinegar, water and herbs. Bring to boil, add mushrooms, and simmer 10 minutes. Cool to serve as a side dish — with rice, for instance. This may be bottled; it keeps several weeks.

Chiles Rellenos (Stuffed Chiles)

The following three recipes use poblano chiles, the big, dark green chiles, either fresh or canned. If you can find fresh poblano chiles, prepare as follows: roast them on a griddle or in a heavy iron skillet, turning often, until skin is charred. Put into a plastic bag, close tightly and wrap in a dish cloth. Let stand for at least 15 minutes, then remove chiles and peel. Slit each chile carefully up the side, leaving top and stem intact, but remove seeds. Chile is now ready to stuff. If using canned chiles, remove seeds and insert stuffing.

Chiles Rellenos de Queso (Chiles Stuffed with Cheese)

6 chiles poblanos or the contents of one 7 oz. can of green chiles
½ lb. Jack cheese
3 Tbsp. flour, plus some for frying

3 eggs, separated
Oil for frying
sauce (see below)

Prepare chiles as above. Cut cheese in thin strips and insert in chiles. Dust with flour. Beat egg whites stiff and fold in egg yolks one by one. Fold three Tbsp. flour into beaten eggs. Dip stuffed, floured chiles in batter and fry quickly in oil until golden brown. Serve with following *sauce*:

1 medium onion, chopped
1 small tomato, chopped
one 10½ oz. can chicken broth

1 clove garlic, minced
2 tomatillos, chopped
salt to taste

Combine and cook until onion is soft. Pour over chiles and serve.

Chiles Filled with Cheeses and Corn

6 chiles poblanos or the contents of one 7 oz. can of green chiles

Filling:

½ cup small curd cottage cheese, drained
¼ cup yogurt
2 eggs, beaten

½ cup Ricotta cheese
1 cup fresh or canned corn, drained

Topping:

1 cup sour cream

¼ cup crumbled Ricotta cheese

Mix together cottage cheese, yogurt, ½ cup Ricotta cheese, corn and eggs. Fill chiles (if fresh, follow preparation instructions above). Arrange in baking dish. Cover with sour cream and sprinkle with ¼ cup Ricotta cheese. Bake in moderate oven (350°) 15 minutes or until filling firms up. Serve immediately. (Chiles may be prepared ahead of time up to point of baking them.)

Chiles Filled with Pork and Pineapple

two 7 oz. cans whole green chiles (there should be six chiles in each can)

Filling:

one 8 oz. can chunk-style pineapple, or one cup fresh pineapple chunks

¼ cup white raisins
1 lb. lean pork, finely chopped
1 medium tomato, chopped
1 clove garlic, minced

¼ cup filberts or pecans, chopped
1 small onion, chopped
chicken broth cubes, instead of salt to taste

Topping:

cinnamon
crème fraîche to cover (see "Notes on Ingredients")

Heat oil, fry finely chopped pork. While pork is frying, add garlic, onion, tomato, and chicken cube seasoning. When pork mixture is fried, set aside to cool, then combine with pineapple, raisins, nuts. Stuff chiles, sprinkle lightly with cinnamon and top with crème fraîche. Serve cold.

EGGS

The two egg recipes which follow are my versions, minus oil, of traditional Mexican recipes.

Huevos Rancheros (Ranch Eggs)

3 cherry tomatoes, peeled and chopped
3 corn tortillas

1 tsp. oregano, crumbled
3 eggs, poached
½ cup canned chiles, chopped

First, make sauce by putting tomatoes, chiles, and oregano in a small pan, cover with water and add salt to taste. Cook slowly 10-15 minutes. Poach eggs and keep warm. Warm tortillas until soft. Place one tortilla on each plate, top with poached egg, and pour sauce over all.

Eggs in Green Chile

2 eggs
1 very small tomato, chopped
3 cups water
2 corn tortillas
salt and pepper to taste

1 oz. canned green chiles, mashed
1 tomatillo, chopped
pinch cumin

Combine chiles, tomato, tomatillo and seasonings in water. Boil slowly until reduced about one-third. Break eggs separately and slip into mixture. Poach to your taste. Serve each egg with some sauce on a tortilla which has been heated.

FISH

Coconut-Lime Fish

Regrettably green coconuts do not seem to be available in the U.S. but, if the opportunity presents itself when in Mexico, don't pass up any of several dishes that make use of the green coconut as the vessel and its milk as the cooking liquid. In the case of fish, there is a tasty coconut casserole of fish and shellfish, with chunks of fish, octopus, shrimp and oysters baked in the milk within the green coconut. However, by using the milk from the brown, ripe coconut, which is more readily available, you can turn out a gourmet fish dish, as follows:

1 whole, mild flavored fish — trout or corbina, for example
1 whole coconut   ½ cup fresh lime juice

Arrange fish in baking pan. Rub inside and out with salt. Remove milk from coconut, add lime juice and beat forcefully with wire whisk to prevent curdling. Pour over fish and bake covered in a 350° oven until fish is flaky, 20 - 25 minutes.

Veracruz Bouillabaisse (My way)

2 lbs. red snapper
1 cup crabmeat
1 lb. shrimp, peeled
1/3 cup olive oil
2 bay leaves
1 red pepper, chopped
1 green pepper, chopped
1/2 tsp. thyme
one 28 oz. can Progresso Italian tomatoes with basil

one 10 oz. can clams (if whole, cut in two)
2 cups onions, sliced
¼ cup parsley, chopped
1 clove garlic, minced
2 Tbsp. fresh fennel, chopped
4 cups water
1 cup sweet sherry

Cut red snapper into strips. Sauté onions in olive oil, add fish, crabmeat, clams, shrimp, tomatoes, bay leaf and water. Bring to boil and cook 15 minutes. Stir in peppers, parsley, garlic, fennel, thyme. Turn heat low. Add sherry. Cover and let simmer 20 minutes over very low heat. To serve, place one slice toasted and buttered French bread in each bowl and ladle soup over bread.

Huachinango a la veracruzana (Red Snapper, Veracruz Style)

    1 whole red snapper, about 4 lbs.
    2 lbs. fresh tomatoes, skinned and mashed
    ¼ cup lime juice   ½ tsp. cumin
    1½ tsp. salt   2 bay leaves
    1 large onion, sliced   3 large cloves garlic, minced
one 7 oz. can green chiles, cut   ¼ cup cooking oil
    into strips   20 green olives
salt to taste   3 Tbsp. capers

Clean red snapper, leaving head and tail on. Prick fish with fork and rub on salt and lime juice. Set in refrigerator for several hours to season. About one hour before serving time, preheat oven to 350°. Fry onion and garlic in oil until clear. Add mashed tomatoes, bay leaves and cumin and simmer for 10 minutes. Pour one-half of the sauce in an ovenproof dish. Lay fish in dish. Add chile strips, capers and olives to remainder of sauce and pour over fish. Bake uncovered about 20 minutes or until fish is just tender. Serve with white rice.

Ceviche (Raw Fish, Marinated Mexican Style)

    2 lbs. mild fish filets, cubed   3 medium tomatoes, chopped
    2 cups fresh lime juice   2 fresh serrano chiles, chopped
    ¾ cup onion, chopped fine   3 Tbsp. salad oil
    1 Tbsp. oregano   ½ cup orange juice
    2 jalapeño chiles, chopped fine,   2 Tbsp. cilantro, chopped
      and 1/4 cup of the pickling   20 green olives
      liquid   avocado slices for garnish

Place fish cubes in a glass bowl, cover with lime juice and leave overnight in the refrigerator. Stir at least twice so cubes will be evenly "cooked." The following day the fish should be white and firm. Drain off lime juice and rinse once with cold water. Add orange juice and rest of ingredients. Allow to season in refrigerator at least two hours. To serve, garnish with avocado slices. Any kind of salt crackers are a good accompaniment. *Note:* This is sheer heresy but if you have an uncontrollable yen for ceviche and lemons are all you can find, use lemon juice. It will change the taste slightly but it's still good.

Beef

Bullfighter's Barbecued Steak

We visited the brave bull breeding ranch at Pastejé in the State of Mexico, and I came home with a beautiful barbecued steak recipe.

3 lbs. top round or boneless rump

1 güero chile, minced	½ cup lemon juice
½ cup orange juice	¼ cup brandy
3 cloves garlic, minced	1 tsp. dried oregano, crushed
¼ cup oil	salt and pepper

Make a marinade of the güero chile (two, if you're *also* brave), orange juice, lemon juice, brandy, garlic, oregano, salt and pepper, and marinate meat at room temperature for four hours. Turn and pierce meat frequently. To barbecue, dry meat, rub oil over surface. Position meat on spit rod — if need be, tie meat securely and run spit through center. Have coals ready and baste frequently with marinade.

Steak Picado

2 lbs. round steak, cut in chunks	1 green pepper, chopped
3 Tbsp. lard, Crisco or oil	1 clove garlic, mashed
1 onion, chopped	3 tomatoes, peeled and mashed

1 tsp. fresh cilantro, minced
1 small serrano or jalapeño chile, seeded and chopped

Brown meat in lard, Crisco or oil. Reduce heat, add pepper, onion, chile, garlic, cilantro, tomatoes, and salt to taste. Cover and simmer until meat is tender, about one hour. If necessary, add a small amount of water.

Goulash Mexicana

4 Tbsp. lard or oil	2 large onions, chopped
1 green pepper, chopped	2 lbs. lean beef, cubed
1 red pepper, chopped	1 Tbsp. paprika
1 Tbsp. cilantro, minced	½ cup red wine
3 oz. canned tomato sauce	6 corn tortillas, quartered and fried

Melt lard (oil), sauté onion until just golden. Add beef and brown. Season to taste and add tomato sauce, cilantro, peppers, paprika, wine, and add water just to cover. Simmer three hours. If more liquid is needed, add more wine. When meat is done, add fried tortilla quarters. Cook five minutes and serve immediaetly.

Pollo a la Olla (Chicken in the Pot)

Pollo a la Olla (Chicken in the Pot)

1 chicken, 4-5 lbs.
1 medium onion, chopped
1 Tbsp. lime juice
½ lb. chorizo, cut in ½ inch
   segments
1 tsp. fresh cilantro, chopped
1 egg, beaten
salt and pepper

1 Tbsp. oil
1½ cups soft white bread
   crumbs
1 tsp. cumin
1 Tbsp. parsley, chopped
1 clove garlic, chopped
1 carrot, 1 onion, pinch of
   thyme

Ready chicken for stuffing. To make stuffing, sauté onion in oil, and mix together with rest of ingredients. In a large soup kettle put the stuffed, well trussed chicken together with the neck, giblets, one carrot, one onion, and pinch of thyme. Cover with water and poach for three hours or until done.

To serve, remove whole chicken and keep warm while guests are consuming the broth. (Have ready 2 Tbsp. chopped green chiles, canned or fresh, for guests to add to the broth as desired.) Cut chicken into pieces and serve each piece with a spoonful or two of the stuffing.

Mexican Chicken Kiev

Mexican Chicken Kiev

4 chicken breasts, boned,
   skinned, and cut in half
½ lb. butter, softened
¼ lb. Jack cheese, crumbled
½ tsp. oregano, crushed
dry bread crumbs and melted butter for breading

one 7 oz. can green chiles,
   chopped
1 tsp. cumin
salt and pepper

Beat chicken breasts flat with cleaver. Mix ½ lb. butter, chiles, cheese, cumin, oregano, salt and pepper. Form into eight balls and chill for one hour. Place one ball in center of each half breast. Roll and secure with toothpick if necessary (butter ball *must* be enclosed). Dip each roll in melted butter, roll in crumbs, and fry in deep fat until brown, 8-10 minutes. Serve with following
sauce:

3 tomatoes, peeled, seeded and
   chopped
¼ cup cilantro, chopped

1 serrano chile, chopped
1 small green onion, chopped

Combine and season with salt.

Cocido de Pollo (Chicken Stew)

1 fryer, 3½ lbs.	4 cherry tomatoes, cut in half
2 cloves garlic	one 7 oz. can pimiento, chopped
1 onion, chopped	1 tsp. oregano, crushed
2 canned green chiles, seeded and diced	
3 Tbsp. pineapple vinegar	3 Tbsp. olive oil
2 Tbsp. sherry	2 bay leaves
1 clove	3 cubes chicken bouillon

Cut up chicken. Put into large soup pot, add rest of ingredients and water to cover. Bring to boil, turn down heat and simmer two hours. Taste and adjust seasoning. Serve with warm tortillas, flour or corn.

Lamb

Asado al Pastor (Shepherd's Roast)

A Shepherd's Roast is prepared in Mexico by barbecuing. I adapted it for the oven. In Mexico, mutton is used; I use lamb.

one 5 lb. leg of lamb, boned and butterflied
10 large avocado leaves (these are musts; no substitutes)
Marinade:

2 Tbsp. olive oil	2 large cloves garlic, minced
1 tsp. oregano	1 tsp. rosemary
8 peppercorns, cracked	1 cup sauterne

Combine marinade ingredients and marinate lamb six hours at room temperature or overnight in the refrigerator. Prepare baking pan by placing in it a flat rack. Put five avocado leaves on rack; lay leg of lamb on avocado leaves and cover with remaining leaves. Bake at 325° until done (allow 30 minutes to pound). Baste frequently with marinade. Serve with *Salsa Borracha* or "Drunken Sauce." (See "Sauces and Seasonings.")

Lamb Shanks Mexicana

6 lamb shanks	1 cup red wine
oil, sufficient for browning	¾ cup onion, minced
1 clove garlic, minced	½ cup fresh cilantro, coarsely
flour, salt and pepper	chopped
1 cup chile pulp (see "Sauces and Seasonings")	

Dredge shanks with flour seasoned with salt and pepper. Heat oil in large Dutch oven and brown shanks slowly on all sides. Add onion, garlic, chile pulp, cilantro and wine. Cover, simmer two hours or until done. Turn shanks occasionally. Serve with mashed potatoes spiced to your taste with chopped, canned green chiles.

Wild Pig Mazatlán

First catch your peccary* and if that isn't feasible, buy a pork loin at your local butcher shop.

1 pork loin, 5 lbs.	4 Tbsp. achiote paste (see
2 large cloves garlic	"Notes on Ingredients")
2 tsp. oregano	½ tsp. cumin
2 tsp. salt	

Crush cloves of garlic with salt, oregano, cumin, and achiote paste, and coat pork loin. Roast slowly at 350° for three hours or until meat thermometer registers 170°. If you'd rather barbecue it, have meat boned, rolled and tied. Season it as above. Place on spit. At 170° it is done.

* If you live in the state of Sinaloa, the peccary can be hunted (one per season) in any uninhabited area. But be careful, he is brave and formidable.

Incredible Roast Pork

one 5 lb. pork loin	2 Tbsp. achiote paste
½ cup papaya, mashed	2 Tbsp. piloncillo, crushed or 2
1 tsp. prepared mustard	Tbsp. brown sugar
1 clove garlic, minced	½ cup coconut cream or 1 cup
1 cup dry sherry	coconut milk
	1 tsp. salt

Score meat. Mix achiote, papaya, piloncillo (brown sugar), mustard, garlic, and salt, and coat the loin with the resulting paste. Mix together coconut cream or milk and sherry. Pour over loin and marinate overnight. Roast in 325° oven until thermometer registers 170°.

Pork Leg Mexicana

one 3½ lb. pork leg	½ cup achiote paste moistened
1 garlic clove, mashed	with lime juice only
1 can beer	2 Tbsp. oil
flour, salt and pepper	

Mash garlic with achiote paste and lime juice. Rub well into meat. Pat flour all over. Brown meat in oil in a Dutch Oven. Add beer, cover and simmer until meat is done — one to two hours. If necessary, add more beer. Slice and serve with green tomato or green chile sauce (see "Sauces and Seasonings").

Cochinita Pibil (Barbecued Pork, Yucatecan style)

This is an easy and mouthwatering party dish. It should be served with black beans, red onion rings (see below), and warm tortillas.

one 5 lb. pork shoulder (with bone, if possible)
1½ packages achiote paste (about 6 oz.), mixed with the juice of one large orange and two limes, 1 Tbsp. vinegar, 1 Tbsp. oil

1 one-inch stick of cinnamon	10 whole cloves
10 green peppercorns	10 black peppercorns
1 Tbsp. oregano	1 Tbsp. salt
6 cloves garlic	oil for frying

banana leaves, IF AT ALL POSSIBLE, sufficient to wrap up the meat (aluminum foil may be used)

With mortar and pestle, or with the flat of a large knife, crush cinnamon, cloves, peppercorns, garlic, oregano, and salt. Blend spices with achiote paste, prepared as above. Score meat deeply and place in a pyrex dish. Pour achiote-spice mixture over meat. Allow to marinate for at least three hours, preferably overnight, checking when possible to see that all meat is covered. Allow five hours for final preparations. Fry achiote covered meat until achiote changes from dull to golden red. Wrap in banana leaves (aluminum foil will serve the purpose but some flavor is lost as well as some of the spectacle). Prepare a Dutch Oven by placing water in the bottom and then a rack (water should just touch not cover rack). Place wrapped up meat on the rack, cover tightly and cook over low heat until meat is done. Try not to remove lid until near the end of the cooking process. It will take about four hours. Meat should be so tender it falls from bone.

Red Onion Rings:

2 medium red onions, sliced thin
1½ cup mild white vinegar or part vinegar, part water

1 tsp. salt	1 tsp. oregano
10 peppercorns	1 habanero chile or 1 serrano chile, finely chopped

Place sliced onions in a sieve, pour boiling water over them and allow to drain. Place them in a glass bowl with the vinegar, chopped chile, and spices. Allow to stand for at least three hours before serving. These can even be made several days ahead; time only improves their flavor.

Fresh Ham a la Mexicana

one 4 lb. fresh ham	1 quart fresh squeezed orange juice
1 cup bottled lime juice	2 cloves garlic, minced
1 tsp. oregano	½ tsp. cumin
2 tsp. salt	

Marinate fresh ham overnight in orange juice, lime juice and spices. Baste occasionally. To bake, drain (reserve marinade), place in baking pan and bake two hours at 350°. Baste with marinade three or four times during baking. Serve with the following *sauce:*

one 14½ oz. can chicken broth
one 4 oz. can green chiles, chopped
1 large onion   1 clove garlic, minced
1 jalapeño chile, chopped   fresh cilantro to taste
1 cup raw tomatillos, papery covering removed, chopped

Blend all ingredients except cilantro. Add salt to taste. Chop cilantro and garnish sauce.

Special Meat Dishes

Manchamanteles (Tablecloth Spotter)

 2 lbs. lean pork, cut in small chunks .
1½ oz. ancho chile, stems and seeds removed
 ½ cup roasted unsalted peanuts or ½ cup unsalted peanut butter
 1 small stick cinnamon   4 whole allspice
 3 whole cloves   2 green onions, chopped
1½ Tbsp. sesame seed   2 garlic cloves, minced
 ¾ lb. tomatoes   4 Tbsp. oil
 2 thick slices fresh pineapple, cubed
 2 plantains (or four green bananas), cut in thick rounds
 2 green apples, unpeeled, cut in 12 slices
 ¾ lb. sweet potatoes, parboiled until nearly tender, skin removed, and cut in thick rounds

Boil pork in five cups of water (salt as you wish) until nearly tender. Reserve broth.

To make sauce, fry ancho chile in oil. Remove. In remaining oil fry peanuts, cinnamon, cloves, allspice, green onions, garlic, and sesame seed until sesame seed just begins to brown. If peanut butter is used, do not fry with spices but add when blending. Blend chile-spices-peanut mixture with tomatoes and one cup pork broth. Fry the mixture again (some oil should still be left from the chile-spice frying, but if not, add a Tbsp. of oil) for five minutes, then slowly add rest of pork broth.

Combine pork, fried chile mixture and all of the fruit except the apples. Cover, bake in 350° oven about 30 minutes or until pork is tender. You may stop the cooking at this point and reheat to serve hours or a day later. When reheating, or if you haven't stopped the cooking, add the apples five minutes before removing baking dish from oven.

83

Sonora Stew

1 lb. chicken, cut up	2 green bananas, cut in quarters
½ lb. beef, cut in chunks	1 cup canned garbanzos
½ lb. pork, cut in chunks	¾ cup onion, chopped
1 large carrot, chopped	2 ears corn, each cut in 6 rounds
½ cup chile pulp (see "Sauces and Seasonings")	juice of one lime, salt and pepper
1 Anaheim green chile, chopped	

Place chicken, beef and pork in stew pot, cover with water, add salt and pepper to taste and simmer until tender. Add onions, garbanzos, carrot, corn and chiles. Add bananas at last minute and simmer gently until tender. Correct seasoning; add salt, if necessary. Just before serving, add lime juice.

Chorizo

Mexican *chorizo* or sausage is moist and lightly piquant in contrast to the rather heavy, hard Spanish version. Homemade chorizo does not have to be put into casings but can be stored in a covered container in the refrigerator, or frozen.

Chorizo Toluca-style

2 lbs. pork tenderloin
2 oz. guajillo chiles (these smooth, red, dried chiles are available at most specialty stores)   ¼ lb. *fresh,* not rendered pork fat
30 cloves garlic, peeled   ½ cup mild white vinegar
2½ tsp. salt

Grind meat and fat together in a coarse grind or have your butcher do it for you. Remove stems from chiles and place in a pan with water to cover. Bring to a quick boil, then remove chiles from pan and squeeze out all water. Put chiles, garlic, salt and vinegar into blender and whirl to a thin paste. Add more vinegar if needed — the chile mixture must be liquid enough to penetrate all of the meat but not so watery that it will separate from it. Add the chile mixture to the ground pork, mix well, then extend the sausage thinly over a large platter to dry out and season for 48 hours. Before using in quantity, fry a little to check on seasoning and, if necessary, correct.

Chorizo Sonora-style

2 lbs. pork, coarse ground with 10-12 cloves garlic

1 tsp. salt	1 tsp. pepper
¼ tsp. cloves	1 Tbsp. oregano
1 tsp. sugar	½ cup paprika
¼ cup chile powder	1 Tbsp. cinnamon (yes, the right amount)
½ cup apple cider or wine vinegar	

Mix paprika with meat. Mix vinegar with all other spices. Combine vinegar-spice mixture with meat-paprika mixture. Spread out on large plate and let season for 24 hours, if necessary longer, until it is dry and well aired.

VEGETABLES

Tomatoes a la Mexicana

6 medium tomatoes
2 cloves garlic, finely minced
1 Tbsp. fresh cilantro, chopped

6 Tbsp. olive oil
1½ cups bread crumbs

Cut the tops off the tomatoes and squeeze out seeds. Salt and cook lightly, cut side down, in olive oil to which you have added garlic cloves. Cook two to three minutes. Remove tomatoes. Add to juices in skillet the bread crumbs and sauté until crumbs are brown and oil absorbed. Remove from fire. Add chopped cilantro. Stuff tomatoes, sprinkle buttered crumbs over tops and put under broiler for a few minutes. Sometimes I char the top. Gives it flavor. I did it once by mistake. Tasted so good I keep on doing it.

Chayotes with Chile and Cheese

4 chayotes
4 oz. Jack cheese, shredded
1 green onion, minced
salt and pepper

4 canned green chiles, seeded and
chopped
2 Tbsp. butter

Peel and slice chayotes crosswise (about ¼ inch thick). Melt butter, add chayotes, onions and chiles. Cover tightly and cook over low flame until chayote is tender. Place in flat baking dish, top with cheese and broil until cheese melts.

Stuffed Zucchini

4 zucchini
1 Tbsp. oil
¼ tsp. cumin
pinch nutmeg

2 Tbsp. minced onion
2 canned green chiles, chopped
¼ tsp. salt
¾ cup grated cheese, your choice

Cut zucchini in half lengthwise, scoop out pulp, sprinkle shells with a little salt, turn upside down and drain. Sauté onion lightly, add chiles, cumin, salt and cheese (reserve some cheese for topping), pulp and nutmeg. Fill shells, top with cheese, place in pan with ⅛ inch water and bake 30 minutes at 350°.

Finger Salad

Take strips of jicama, celery and cucumber. Salt and coat with olive oil. Sprinkle with chile powder.

My Cucumber Salad

1 large cucumber
2 Tbsp. pistacho nuts, chopped

½ cup sour cream
½ tsp. cumin

Slice cucumber paper thin. Marinate in the sour cream mixed with pistacho nuts and cumin.

BEANS

Since beans are served near the end of most Mexican meals, we'll put them here although some of the recipes given below are meals in themselves.

While an *olla* or clay pot is desirable for cooking Mexican beans, it is not indispensable; good beans can be made in a pressure cooker.

Note: beans are *not* soaked prior to cooking, but started in cold water.

Basic Recipe

1 lb. beans
2 quarts water
2 Tbsp. oil

1 Tbsp. salt
½ onion or several green onion tops

Put everything together into pressure cooker. Cooking time depends on altitude; see your cooker instruction folder.

When the beans are cooked, body is often given to the broth and additional flavor to the beans by "frying" — not to be confused with "refrying" (see below). Chopped onions are fried in a small amount of oil or lard in a cooking pot (again, a clay vessel is preferred but not absolutely necessary); a few cooked beans are mashed therein with a fork, and fried; the rest of the beans and broth are added and then left to simmer 10 to 15 minutes.

Refried Beans (Frijoles Refritos)

In blender put a quart of cooked beans with sufficient broth to blend easily. Barely turn blender on and off, to leave some of the beans in a semiwhole state. Heat four or five tablespoons of oil, depending upon dryness of beans and amount of oil added in cooking beans originally. In short, use your judgement and more oil than you think you should. Fry two tablespoons of chopped onion in the oil until onion is clear. Add beans and stir until they are dry and can be formed into a roll. Experts do it with a flapjack technique but you can cheat by gently tipping the frying pan back and forth, once the bean mixture is sufficiently dry. Adorn the roll with triangles of fried tortillas and slender cheese wedges. Any kind of bean may be used. Either use as a side dish or as an appetizer.

BEAN MEALS

Frijoles Puercos

I have never been sure whether the name of this bean dish translates as "Pork Beans" since most of the additions are pork products, or whether it might be "Pig Beans" since some cooks go so far as to add sardines, sliced avocados, hardboiled eggs, etc. I choose *Pork Beans*.

Follow the basic bean recipe (using any but black beans), and when beans are about ¾ cooked, add the following in equal, reasonable proportions, with beans ending up in the majority:

small pieces of raw pork meat with bones
pieces of cracklings
segments of chorizo (spicy Italian sausage might be substituted)
1 or more pasilla chiles, depending on your endurance

Allow all of the above to simmer until beans finish cooking. When serving, have ready the following in small dishes so that each person can garnish the beans as he chooses:

chopped onions
fresh cilantro, chopped
fresh green chiles, chopped

chopped radishes
oregano, crushed

Frijoles Norteños (Beans, Northern Style)

2 lbs. red kidney beans
8 oz. ham, cubed
1 lb. chorizo
3 large onions, sliced
½ cup tequila
¼ cup canned serrano or
 jalapeño chiles, chopped

6 oz. bacon cut into strips
1 lb. leftover roast pork, cubed
2 lbs. tomatoes, chopped
three 8 oz. bottles beer
½ tsp. each oregano, marjoram,
 rosemary

Cook beans in pressure cooker with two quarts water until skin just starts to wrinkle (about 20 minutes). Remove beans and broth. In a large casserole fry bacon and sausage. Add onions and brown, then add tomato. Add rest of ingredients, including beans and broth, except tequila. Let simmer until beans are tender. Add tequila a few minutes before serving.

Enfrijoladas (Corn tortillas dipped in thick, hot bean broth and folded in half)

An excellent accompaniment for huevos rancheros or any other egg (meat) dish with a piquant sauce. Calculate about ½ cup thick bean broth per tortilla, and usually two enfrijoladas per person. Prepare bean broth by puréeing beans in blender, and frying resulting mixture in a small amount of oil until it is the consistency of a medium thick white sauce. This can be done ahead of time but the enfrijoladas should be assembled just before serving.

bean broth	corn tortillas
onion, chopped	Mexican white cheese, crumbled

Have bean broth simmering over low flame. Fry tortillas. One by one, dip tortillas into broth and fold over. Remove with spatula to individual plates or serving platter, previously heated. Garnish each enfrijolada with one scant tablespoon each of chopped onion and crumbled cheese.

SAUCES AND SEASONINGS

While all cooked sauces are prepared in Mexico by frying, I have made some close approximations using very little or no oil.

Salsa de Tomatillo (Green Tomato Sauce)

½ cup water	½ lb. tomatillos
1 fresh serrano chile	1 clove garlic
¼ tsp. salt	1 tsp. fresh cilantro, chopped

Remove papery covering from tomatillos and chop. Place tomatillos and chile in saucepan with water and cook for 10 minutes. Mash garlic with salt and cilantro. Put in blender together with cooked tomatillos and purée.

Salsa de Jitomate (Red Tomato Sauce)

1 lb. tomatoes, peeled and chopped	1 clove garlic
	½ tsp. oregano
¼ tsp. salt	1 serrano chile, minced

Mash garlic with salt, oregano and chile. Put in saucepan with tomatoes (no water) and cook slowly for 10 minutes. Mash thoroughly. Sauce should be thick.

Green Chile Sauce

1 medium onion, chopped	1 clove garlic, minced
1 cup tomatoes, chopped	½ cup canned green chiles, chopped
¼ tsp. cumin	
1 cup water	2 sprigs cilantro
	salt to taste

Mix all ingredients together in saucepan and cook slowly until onion and tomato are done.

Salsa Borracha (Drunken Sauce)

This is traditionally made with pulque but since that beverage is not available outside Mexico, tequila is an acceptable substitute.

6 pasilla chiles	¾ cup water
¾ cup fresh orange juice	½ cup olive oil
2 tsp. salt	¼ cup tequila
1 onion, chopped fine	Mexican white cheese

Barely parch chiles. Remove stems and seeds and simmer in orange juice and water until soft. Drain off most of liquid. Put in blender with salt, tequila, olive oil and blend until smooth. Put into serving dish. Crumble cheese. Sprinkle chopped onion and crumbled cheese over surface of sauce.

Hot Jalapeño Sauce

1 large garlic clove, minced	1 large or 2 small jalapeño chiles
½ tsp. salt	2 Tbsp. hot chicken broth
3 Tbsp. salad oil	1 Tbsp. bread crumbs, moistened and squeezed dry

Mash together garlic, chile(s) and salt. Add bread crumbs, then add the oil, stirring constantly. Thin with *hot* chicken broth.

Chile Paste

1 lb. dried red chiles (preferably ancho chiles)

Remove stems and seeds. Cut up and put in large saucepan with water to cover. Bring to boil and simmer 20-25 minutes. When chiles are soft, drain and purée in blender. Paste should be very thick. I put it in a plastic container and freeze it, thawing each time I want some and refreezing the rest. Makes about three cups.

Guacamole

This sauce-appetizer, which derives it name from the Aztec word for avocado (*auacatl*), can assume many guises — mashed, chopped or blended — but the only basic difference is whether tomato is added or not. The other ingredients remain the same: avocado, onion, green chiles and cilantro.

If the avocado is firm, you might chop it together with onion, tomato, green chiles and cilantro in the following proportions, give or take your preferences:

1 medium avocado	2 green onions
1 small tomato	1 serrano chile
1 tsp. cilantro	salt to taste

Or the guacamole may be made with mortar and pestle (and served in the mortar). In that case:

1 medium avocado, good and
  ripe
1 serrano chile
1 tsp. cilantro, chopped

2 green onions
1 tomatillo, fresh or canned
salt to taste

Remove husk from tomatillo, if fresh; chop coarsely. Chop *one* green onion, and the chile; then diligently mash onion, chile and tomatillo with about ¼ tsp. salt, in mortar. Add avocado and mix well. Top with remaining green onion, chopped fine, and cilantro. The tomatillo can be omitted but it serves two purposes: to maintain the true green color of the avocado longer, and two, it heightens the taste of the avocado.

You may, if time presses, substitute a blender for the mortar and pestle. The guacamole then will be thinner and creamier.

Salsa de Esperanza (My friend Hope's sauce)

(all chiles are fresh except the pasilla chile)

2 Anaheim green chiles
3 güero chiles
2 pasilla chiles
1 tsp. oregano
1 Tbsp. cilantro, coarsely
  chopped
salt to taste

2 jalapeño chiles
7 serrano chiles
1 large clove garlic
1 green onion
one 12 oz. can V-8 vegetable
  juice cocktail

Roast fresh chiles (all except pasilla) on griddle or in iron skillet, turning frequently. When evenly charred, put them into a plastic bag, close it tightly and wrap in a dish cloth. Allow to stand 15 minutes, then peel, leaving in seeds or not depending on how hot you want the sauce. Parch pasilla (place on hot griddle for five seconds each side). Chop chiles, garlic, onion, and add them to heated V-8 juice together with oregano and cilantro. Cook for five minutes. Cool to serve.

A good *barbecue sauce*

½ cup vinegar
  2 Tbsp. sugar
  2 Tbsp. lime juice
1½ Tbsp. Worcestershire sauce

¼ cup catsup
  2 Tbsp. garlic, mashed
  1 tsp. soy sauce

Mix together all ingredients.

.Seasoning Ideas

To mashed potatoes I add green chile pulp to taste. I make the pulp from canned green chiles (seed the chiles and mash and mash). I do the same with baked potatoes, adding chile pulp with the butter after I have fractured the potatoes.

Add 1 Tbsp. tequila to your guacamole.

When your baked ham is almost done, coat it with guava jelly; then continue baking until done.

When serving rice (the quantity in the basic recipe), add one Tbsp. achiote paste mixed with two Tbsp. melted butter just before presentation. Good!

Try adding epazote (it grows wild in California) to your next pot of black beans or other gas-producing food. It is an effective antiflatulent.

FRUITS PREPARED AS SIDE DISHES

Fried Green Bananas

4 large green bananas
¼ cup oil

½ cup brown sugar
cinnamon

Select bananas as green as possible. Peel and cut in half lengthwise. Heat ¼ cup oil in skillet, moderate heat, and fry bananas on each side three to four minutes until tender and brown. Sprinkle with brown sugar and a dash of cinnamon. Serve as a side dish with refried beans.

Baked Papaya

1 firm medium size papaya
lime juice

shredded coconut, sweetened or
unsweetened

Cut papaya in half, leave skin on but remove seeds. Fill papaya halves with shredded coconut, sprinkle with lime juice and bake at 350° for 20 minutes.

If you don't wish to fill it with coconut, you may bake the papaya, halved and seeded, without a filling, and serve it with melted butter, salt and pepper.

Papaya prepared either way is an excellent accompaniment for meats, instead of potatoes or rice.

DESSERTS

Piña Cocada (Pineapple Coconut Pudding)

2 cups canned pineapple juice
2½ Tbsp. cornstarch
1 tsp. vanilla

2 cups moist coconut
3 Tbsp. sugar
pinch salt

Mix cornstarch with sugar, slowly add pineapple juice to make a smooth paste, then add rest of juice. Cook over moderate heat, stirring constantly until thick and smooth. Add coconut, vanilla and salt. Chill well before serving.

Coconut Pudding

Take a whole coconut, puncture the eyes, drain out milk, and split open (I use a machete); sun or oven-dry meat until it can be grated. If you do not wish to go to this trouble, buy shredded dry coconut, and canned coconut milk.

3 cups grated coconut
3 Tbsp. cornstarch
pinch salt

1½ cups coconut milk
3 Tbsp. sugar

Mix cornstarch and sugar, add coconut milk and grated coconut, and boil. Stir constantly. When thick, pour into dish and cool.

This also makes an excellent filling for a *Coconut Cake*. Make a light white cake (package mix is fine), substituting coconut milk for the plain milk. Fill with coconut pudding, frost with whipped cream and sprinkle with grated coconut.

Limones Rellenos de Coco (Candied Limes Filled with Coconut)

Preparation time: four days (but worth it)

10 limes
1¼ lbs. sugar

½ Tbsp. detergent
2 cups grated coconut

Cut a cross in top of limes. Put limes in water to cover, add ½ Tbsp. detergent and bring to boil. Cool, drain. Work very carefully and, through split tops, separate pulp from peel. Pull out pulp and wash lime shell carefully. Leave in cold water 24 hours.

Combine 1½ cups water and ¾ lb. sugar and bring to a boil. Boil until thick. Add drained limes and cook over low heat 30 minutes. Let stand in syrup overnight. Next day, boil for 30 minutes. Let stand in syrup overnight. Following day, boil again for 30 minutes. By this time the limes should be tender and penetrated with syrup. Combine ½ lb. sugar, ½ cup water and bring to boil. Add coconut and cook until syrup is absorbed. Drain limes and stuff with coconut. *Buena suerte!*

Flan de Tres Leches (Three Milk Custard)

Preheat oven to 350°.

1 can evaporated milk
1 can condensed milk
pinch salt

1¾ cups homogenized milk
8 eggs
1 tsp. each vanilla and orange
extract

Prepare your mold coated with caramelized sugar (I use a two-quart ovenproof pyrex bowl). Put ½ cup sugar into small pan over low heat. Cook, stirring constantly with a wooden spatula until sugar caramelizes. Pour into mold and rapidly swirl around sides of mold to cover as completely as possible. Set aside to cool.

Put milks, eggs, salt and flavorings into blender and let fly for one minute. Pour mixture into caramel coated mold. Never mind if it crackles and pops. Cover tightly with aluminum foil. Put into a larger pan with water; water should reach up to about halfway on bowl sides. Bake 1½ hours at 350°. Allow custard to cool completely in oven. (I do this last thing at night and allow the custard to cool in the oven overnight). Put in refrigerator at least one hour before unmolding on large plate with upturned sides (the caramelized sugar will have turned to syrup and this type of plate will keep you from making a mess).

Wild Lime Pie

If you can find wild limes, good. If not, buy limes at the market.

2 large limes, washed and cut into small pieces, rind and all

1¾ cups sugar	¼ cup butter
1 Tbsp. flour	1 Tbsp. cornstarch
⅛ tsp. salt	pastry for a two-crust pie

5 large eggs, lightly beaten (before beating, use a small amount of the egg white to brush over bottom pie crust)

Place limes in food processor with chopping blade in place; chop as finely as possible (or can be put in blender for 30 seconds). Place in glass bowl, add sugar, and let stand three hours. Mix flour, cornstarch and salt, add melted butter slowly to make smooth paste. Add to lime-sugar mixture. Beat eggs lightly and add. Pour mixture into unbaked pie shell (brushed with egg white), and cover with top crust. Brush with milk and sprinkle with sugar. Bake at 325° for one hour. Cool before serving.

DOROTHY'S SPECIALS

Pimiento with Cheese

one 3 oz. pkg. cream creese	one 7 oz. can sweet red pimientos, shredded
½ cup sugar	
¼ cup water	¼ cup vinegar

Bring to boil sugar, vinegar and water. Add shredded pimientos and cool. Pour over brick of cream cheese. Serve with crackers.

Cornish Hens, My Way

3 Cornish hens	½ tsp. ground black pepper
1 oz. achiote paste	salt to taste

3 large onions, boiled and soaked in sauterne or other dry white wine overnight

Stuff hens with onions. Mix black pepper with achiote paste and salt. Grease bird thoroughly with oil and rub all over with the achiote mixture. Broil or barbecue until golden brown and tender. Cut each bird in half to serve.

Higos Reales (Royal Figs)

1 lb. dried figs	1½ cups port
½ cup sauterne	¼ cup brown sugar
½ tsp. cinnamon	¼ tsp. cloves
1 tsp. grated orange rind	1 tsp. grated lemon rind
½ cup Brazil nuts, chopped	crème fraîche (see "Notes on Ingredients")

Mix all ingredients except Brazil nuts and crème fraîche, and simmer for one hour. Allow to stand at room temperature overnight. Refrigerate following day. Serve (six servings) topped with crème fraîche and chopped Brazil nuts.

Almond-Cheese Dip for Tortilla Strips

fried corn tortilla strips (about one inch wide)
1½ cups almonds, toasted and slivered

3 oz. cream cheese	3 oz. blue cheese

Blend almonds and cheeses thoroughly in food processor or blender, and you're ready to dip.

Jellied Wine Salad

2 envelopes unflavored gelatin	2 cups any sweet wine (Tokay,
2 cups water	Marsala, Madeira, Sherry, Port,
¼ cup sugar	sweet Sauterne, etc.)
¼ tsp. salt	

Mix gelatin with water and heat slowly until gelatin is dissolved. Remove from heat and add wine, sugar and salt. Pour into glass dish 8" x 8" x 2" and chill. Cut into squares, place on lettuce leaves and top each square with a dollop of sour cream. Very good as an accompaniment for meat, a change from applesauce, etc.

For the attitude adjustment hour, here is an offering of

DRINKS, SOFT AND OTHERWISE

Aguas Frescas (Refreshing Waters)

Many fruits, alone or in combination, whirled in a blender can be used to make aguas frescas: a glass of orange juice, several slices of fresh pineapple, three glasses of water, one-third cup sugar, and you have more than a quart of delicious beverage. Apples, peaches, melon, plums, pears, papaya, mango are all susceptible to blending. A few drops of lime or lemon juice heightens the flavor. However, there is one such beverage that might not occur to you. so herewith the recipe for:

Horchata de Arroz con Semillas de Melón (Orgeat of Rice with Cantaloupe Seeds)

1/3 cup rice	3 two-inch sticks, cinnamon
1/2 cup cantaloupe seeds	1 cup sugar
6 cups water	1 thick wedge of cantaloupe

Soak rice overnight in water, together with cinnamon. Following day, remove cinnamon, and blend rice, cantaloupe seeds, cantaloupe wedge and sugar in sufficient water to blend easily. To serve, add rest of water, stick cinnamon, and one cup crushed ice.

Teshuin de Piña (Pineapple Cider)

This beverage is betwixt and between soft and otherwise so serves as a good transition for this section.

rind of one pineapple cut so quite a bit of fruit remains sticking to it
1 stick cinnamon   1½ cups dark brown sugar
2 quarts water

Let everything stand together in a glass or crockery jar, until it *just* begins to ferment — three or four days. Strain and pasteurize (hold at boiling point for seven minutes). Chill to serve.

Note 1: Teshuin is the name common in northern Mexico; it is called tepache in central Mexico, Guadalajara south.

Note 2: If you add tamarind pods to the mixture while steeping, the result is called *garapiña,* and it's still more delicious.

Note 3: If you use teshuin/tepache as a mixer for tequila, you have a rousing drink (lots of crushed ice should be added). As far as I know, it's my own invention and as yet unnamed although we might call it *Tetepache,* not just for the combination of the ingredients' names but because you stutter after two.

Speaking of tequila and such, here are several "invents," as one of my Mexican friends calls them:

Tequila Surprise

6 cups cider   2 cups tequila
1 slice lime and one cinnamon stick (for stirrer) for each portion

Heat cider, add tequila. Pour into mugs, garnish and serve immediately. (Wait for a cold night.)

Piña Tequila

2 oz. coffee cream   4 oz. pineapple juice
3 oz. tequila

Put in blender with ice cubes for one minute.

Promise of Delight

4 oz. pineapple juice
1 oz. light rum

3 oz. tequila
2 oz. coconut cream, canned

Mix with 10-15 ice cubes for one minute. Strain and serve in tall glass.

Taxco Tango

2 jiggers tequila
1 tsp. honey

1 jigger lime juice
ice, club soda to fill tall glass

Shake well.

Tequila Moonrise

1 egg white
3 oz. tequila

1½ tsp. sugar
1½ tsp. lime juice

Put all ingredients in blender with three ice cubes for 30 seconds or shake vigorously 12 times in a bar shaker. Strain into glass.

Sí, Sí, Señora (12 portions)

12 jiggers tequila
 2 sprigs fresh mint, chopped
 2 Tbsp. cinnamon

grated rind, four limes
12 each, black peppercorns and
 whole cloves, finely ground

Combine, cover and let stand overnight. To serve, add:

2 jiggers Triple Sec
6 Tbsp. sugar dissolved in *very little* boiling water

6 jiggers port

Serve ice cold garnished with green cherries.

Naranjada

1½ oz. fresh orange juice

1½ oz. tequila

Put in blender with lots of ice and serve frozen.

Bul

And for the morning after, as devised by a Mexican friend. It's so refreshing you'll be making more than one pitcher.

glass pitcher (one quart)
1 jigger rum
1 jigger brandy
1 jigger gin
1 jigger vodka

2/3 cup simple syrup
2/3 cup lime juice
1/2 bottle club soda
one 8 oz. bottle Mexican beer
ice cubes

In pitcher, mix together lime juice, simple syrup, gin, rum, vodka, brandy. Add beer, club soda, and sufficient ice cubes to fill pitcher. Stir gently until mixture is frigid. Serve.

Café de Olla

An anticlimax but you can always add a dollop of brandy. **Properly, this coffee should be made in an** *olla* **or clay pot.**

2 quarts water   1 cup dark brown sugar
4 two-inch sticks cinnamon   6 heaping Tbsp. coffee, coarse
     grind

Boil water with sugar and cinnamon until sugar is dissolved and cinnamon is fragrant. Add coffee, allow to come to a boil, turn off and let steep five minutes.

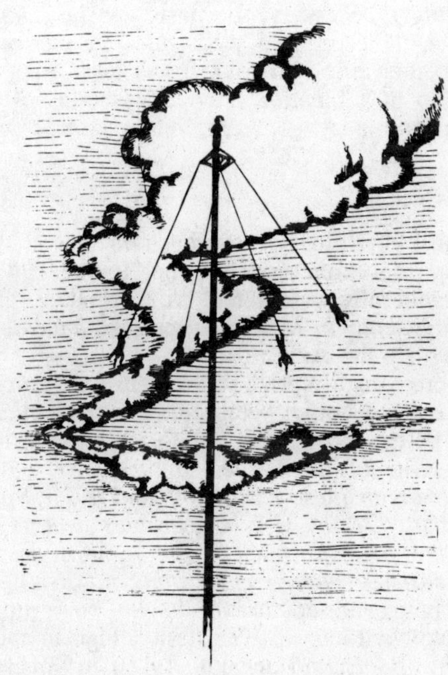

NOTES ON INGREDIENTS

Mexican cooking depends in large part for its special flavor on certain ingredients once found principally in Mexico but now a part of the world food basket. Herewith a few notes about some of them.

Achiote

The seeds of the achiote (*Bixa orellana*) tree yield a flavoring used particularly in Yucatecan cooking. The orange red seeds are processed to obtain a paste which is used as the basis for sauces for meat and fish. The soft brick of paste is usually available in packages (about four ounces) in the Mexican section of supermarkets and specialty stores. If absolutely necessary, the paste can be made from seeds as follows: for each tablespoon of seeds, use one cup of water. Boil for 10 minutes and then allow to soak for at least four hours. Grind as finely as possible in a blender. Two tablespoons of seeds are about the equivalent of one package. Achiote may also be sold as "Annato."

Avocados

Native to most of tropical America, and one of the New World's most interesting and exotic contributions to the Old World's menus, avocados are generally associated with Mexico, probably because of the name: *aguacate* in Mexican Spanish; *auacatl* in Nahuatl, the language spoken by the Aztecs.

Avocados were a highly prized food item long before the Spaniards arrived, and had not only been cultivated as such but probably improved by native horticulturists through selection of the best fruiting forms. One of the earliest Spanish friar-chroniclers wrote: *Among many fruits in these mountains and in all New Spain there is one called* auacatl. *On the tree it resembles a large fig although the flavor is like that of pine nuts... the Indians abstain from eating it during their fasts because it is rich and nourishing.*

And, as if being an epicurean delight were not sufficient, the avocado is a medicinal marvel. The flesh is high in energy components and Vitamin B; the ground-up skin, taken in sweetened water, is a speedy expellant of intestinal parasites; the seeds, ground and mixed with bone marrow, are used to treat dandruff and to promote hair growth; and the ground-up seed alone is used to poison mice. The smooth flesh is also reputed to be an aphrodisiac but this may be a consequence of a common phenomenon in herbal medicine where a therapeutic property is ascribed to a plant because of some outstanding physical trait —color, form, aroma, etc.— and one of the Aztec names for testicle was auacatl, an accurate description of the fruit's

and some random thoughts on food in Mexico

appearance. The tree is of a noble family, the laurel, which includes the *Laurus nobilis* used by the Romans to crown their great, and the cinnamon, camphor, and sassafras trees. But the only one bearing edible fruit is the avocado.

Beans

Together with corn, squash and chile, beans are Mexico's most ancient food. In the thousands of years that Mexicans have been preparing beans, they have acquired a few tricks. Not only have they developed many bean dishes, but they manage to make the simple boiled bean an every-meal pleasure. The fastest cooking bean is a pale yellow variety called *canario;* the slowest, the black or *frijol negro.* The color range between these two extremes is almost total: bright yellow, pink, red, purple, brown, and several mottled varieties.

Four seasonings are commonly used with beans: oregano, cilantro, cumin (in northern Mexico), and epazote (only with black beans). In Veracruz and along the Gulf Coast, where a particularly succulent variety of black bean is grown, a popular dish is *moros y cristianos* (Moors and Christians), black beans and white rice. Actually an adaptation of a Cuban dish, it is frequently served with fried bananas, and accompanied by a sauce of chopped tomatoes, onions, and small fresh green chiles.

Chayote

A mild flavored vegetable, growing in popularity and now cultivated in the southern United States, the chayote was known and widely used by the Indian peoples of the American continent long before the arrival of the Spaniards. Shaped somewhat like a large pear, there are several varieties, ranging in color from dark to light green. Some are smooth and some covered with spines. While it is usual in Mexico to boil them unskinned and then peel them, they are more flavorful and tender if first peeled and then fried or baked — reduces cooking time, too. Chayote can be an interesting addition to a stew, along with carrots, onions, peas, and the more usual vegetables.

Cheese

While many very good cheeses are made in Mexico, the one most often used for garnishing is *queso fresco* or "fresh cheese." It is not as fresh as its name would indicate but rather a semi-dry, white cheese, easily crumbled. With the growing popularity of Mexican food abroad, a similar product has appeared in U.S. markets, often called "Mexican White Cheese" or even "Queso Fresco."

Several of the recipes in this book use Monterey Jack cheese as a substitute for a mild cheddar-type cheese used in Mexico. Monterey Jack is perhaps more easily found in western United States than in eastern where Muenster would be an acceptable substitute.

If traveling in Mexico, don't fail to try the many local cheeses. Notable cheese-making areas are the states of Querétaro, San Luis Potosí, Chihuahua, Oaxaca and Chiapas.

Chiles

Chile is a beautiful and indispensable concept to those who cook or eat Mexican food. At least 30 varieties of *Capsicum annuum* and *Capsicum frutescens* are commonly used in Mexico, and their widely differing flavor, form, color, and degree of piquancy are a delight to the palate and a challenge to the inventive cook.

Given the complexity of the subject, particularly because the same chile may be called by different names in different areas and, equally, the same name may be given to different chiles (e.g. the pasilla chile of Oaxaca is very different from the one called pasilla in central Mexico), only the chile varieties used in the recipes given in this book will be described.

Serrano. Commonly known as *chilito verde* or "little green chile," the serrano is probably the most frequently used chile, in its fresh state, in Mexico. It is small, usually slender, and on a 1 to 10 scale of hotness would probably win a 9. Serranos are sometimes found canned in a vinaigrette with carrots and onions.

Jalapeño. Sometimes known as *cuaresmeño*, it is a dark green chile, larger and fatter than the serrano. It is often used in a vinaigrette garnish with other vegetables. The very brave eat jalapeños stuffed with cheese, fish or meat. *Chipotli* chiles are ripe jalapeños that have been smoked, becoming brown and wrinkled and increasing in hotness. The fresh jalapeño might be 7-8 on the scale, the smoked or chipotli, 9.

Güero. Blond like its name, long and slender, it is often pickled and canned. Its piquancy varies greatly with region of origin and rainfall. For instance, if grown during the rainy season, it tends to be less hot.

Poblano. The preferred chile for stuffing, the poblano is a large, shiny dark green chile which might rate 5 to 7 on the piquancy scale. Mexicans say that those with crooked stems are hotter than those with straight, the heat being unable to escape through the crook. The *Anaheim* chile, with a 3-4 rating, developed in the United States, is similar in shape and size and can also be used for *chiles rellenos*. As for canned green chiles suitable for stuffing, Ortega is a long established brand and because the chiles are fire- not lye-peeled, their product can be recommended. With the growing popularity of Mexican food, there are now other brands on the market, all of

100

which including Ortega rate no more than a mild 1.

Ancho. Most authorities say the ancho chile is a dried poblano but one very respectable Mexican botanist states that the poblano when dried becomes the *mulato* (a large dark brown, almost black chile). Be that as it may, the deep brick red, dried ancho ("broad") chile may be so named because it is a big chile, wide at the top and through the middle. A frequent base for sauces, it can also be stuffed. Five to 7 might be its range on the piquancy scale.

Pasilla. A long slender, deep brown dried chile, the pasilla has a very distinctive flavor. It can be turned into an interesting garnish by slicing it fine, frying it with a small amount of onion, adding orange juice to cover, and then simmering it until the orange juice is absorbed. Variable in piquancy, perhaps 6 to 8.

Cascabel. Its name means "rattle," but it's a diminutive one, a small shiny, rust colored globe with a piquancy rating of 5 to 7. Usually toasted and ground with spices for sauces.

Guajillo. A dried chile with a red-brown, smooth skin, not wrinkled like that of the pasilla or ancho, the guajillo tends to be long and slender, and is the preferred chile in Mexico for sauces used with lamb and mutton.

Habanero. Ending the list of chiles is the habanero with the reputation of being the hottest chile in Mexico, a 10, of course. It is most used on the Yucatán península. This small, elongated globe ranges in color from pale green to orange depending on the degree of ripeness. It is interesting to note that the only other chile which can rival it in piquancy, the *manzano* ("apple shaped"), is also orange.

Chiles can be grown in the garden or as potted plants. All varieties are highly decorative since the chiles, in all stages of ripeness from green to red or golden, hang together on the plant like ornaments on a Christmans tree Good for the soul, the palate, and any Vitamin C deficiency.

Chocolate

In Mexico, chocolate is little used in cooking. Rather it is a favorite drink, especially for late supper with sweet rolls and/or tamales. The word derives from an Indian word and the drink was a favorite of Aztec rulers.

Cacao, from which chocolate is made, is produced by a tropical tree in six-inch long pods that hold 20 to 40 beans each. Somewhat bigger than a large almond, the beans are covered by a thin skin that comes off in the roasting process. The largest, most perfectly formed beans were used as money by the Indian peoples before the Spanish Conquest. That is why chocolate was drunk only by members of the nobility who were quite literally consuming their capital when they indulged. Before the European versions of chocolate appeared, the Indians had developed some variations in the beverage by adding certain herbs, spices (including vanilla), chile, honey, or corn gruel. Moctezuma II was extremely fond of the beverage, reputedly drinking 50 cups a day. His chefs produced a refined drink, almost pure foam, with the "consistency of honey that dissolved slowly in the mouth." Of course, Moctezuma had the advantage when nearly down to his last bean, of being able to send out his tribute collectors for more baskets full, or his warriors to conquer new cacao tree acreage.

To the prosperous and comfort-loving Spanish religious orders goes the credit for having developed the chocolate beverage we know today. Early in the colonial era they added sugar — sugar cane was introduced by the Spaniards — and cinnamon, sometimes egg yolks, almonds, and dry cake crumbs. Families soon had their favorite recipes, and itinerant women grinders called periodically with their *metates* or large flat grinding stones to prepare several months' chocolate supply for the households. The custom persists in a few areas. Roasted cacao beans and sugar, in about equal proportions by weight, are ground to a smooth paste together with any or all of the other additives mentioned above. The paste is then dried in molds or patted into rounds and wrapped to store.

Chorizo

The making of chorizo or Mexican sausage might, at first thought, be considered a formidable undertaking. But, in these days of food processors, it is quick and easy. And having chorizo — no need to put it in casings — in your refrigerator or freezer, is a guarantee of a quick and tasty solution to feeding unexpected guests or for making a different dish for a Sunday brunch. Take, for instance, scrambled eggs with chorizo (fry the chorizo first, then add the eggs) or try a sprinkling of chorizo on top of enchiladas, which adds a festive touch. Chorizo combined with fried chopped onion, chopped fresh green chiles, and boiled, chopped potatoes makes an excellent taco filling. Two recipes for chorizo are given in the section of meat recipes.

Cilantro

In flower, the cilantro or coriander plant resembles anis, dill, fennel and parsley, as well it might since it too is a member of the Umbelliferae family. The leaves of this herb are used often in fresh sauces to give special flavor, and it is one of the basic herbs in green mole. Its penetrating flavor and aroma make it an herb either heartily liked or disliked.

Cilantro (also sold under the name of "Chinese parsley") is used fresh and does not keep well although it will retain its freshness several days if kept in a plastic bag in the vegetable compartment of the refrigerator. Dried cilantro can be found more readily in U.S. markets. It is somewhat different in flavor, as for instance the difference in flavor between fresh parsley and dried, but may be used in some recipes.

It appears that for the fresh herb the Mexican name cilantro, rather than coriander, has found favor abroad. However, the seeds, with an entirely different flavor, are always referred to as coriander seeds.

Cream

The closest equivalent to the thick, unsweetened cream used in Mexico is crème fraîche, which can be made as follows:

Put two cups whipping cream (unwhipped) in a jar. Add 5-1/2 tablespoons of buttermilk. Cap jar tightly, shake vigorously, and then leave overnight at room temperature. Keep in refrigerator thereafter.

Epazote

While this herb bears an ambrosial botanical name *(Chenopodium ambrosoides)* its common name, epazote, comes from the Nahuatl words *epatl* (skunk) and *tzotl* (filth), vividly descriptive but greatly exaggerated. Its pungent flavor is a must in dishes such as black beans, mushrooms, squash flower soup, brains, and *esquites* (fresh corn fried or steamed with butter, chopped onion, fresh green chile, and epazote).

The small leafed variety, purple of stem and base of leaf, is the most flavorful. It is hardy in all but the bitterest climes and will propagate itself by seed and root to the extreme of becoming a pest. Various medicinal properties are attributed to it, the best known being in the treatment of helminthiasis (worms), undoubtedly the reason for one English common name, "wormseed." It's not the seeds, however, but the leaves that are used in a strong infusion or tea. Its efficacy in this respect has been fairly well proven. In folk medicine, many are the marvelous powers ascribed to it. Supposedly, epazote tea will cause hair to grow on bald heads, cure asthma and St. Vitus dance, calm the nerves and aid digestion, even remedy toothaches.

Flowers

Mexicans make full use of every growing thing. Because for thousands of years they have been experimenting in a search for edible and medicinal plants, they have catalogued and exploited just about every leaf, stem, root, and flower. The few flowers cited here, from the fields of the Central Highlands, are known and eaten by all rural inhabitants.

Most widely used are squash blossoms; the big, deep yellow flowers are prepared by removing the stem and knobby center. If the petals have not been torn, the blossoms are filled with a very mild cheese, dipped into an egg batter, fried, then allowed to simmer for a short time in a tomato sauce spiced with green chile. Squash blossom soup is made by simmering the flowers in chicken broth.

Epazote is a must seasoning, and some type of green chile is added, according to tolerance, As a special touch, strips of fried tortillas and tiny cubes of cheese are added at the time of serving. Squash blossoms are also used as a filling for tacos, as one of the vegetables in meat stews, or in combination with field mushrooms.

Coral tree blossoms are picked while still in bud and prepared for use by boiling (the water in which they are cooked is thrown away, not used as in the case of squash flowers). The buds are very compact and have a nutty flavor. A soup is made by adding them to a light tomato-beef broth, or they too, may be pressed into patties, cheese added, egg-dipped, fried, and served with a tomato sauce.

The blossoms of the yucca tree are treated in the same way, as the coral tree buds. Wild turnip blooms and greens are fried and eaten in tacos or quesadillas. Even the flowers of the maguey or agave — century plant, as it is more commonly known in English — are used, usually in egg patties. Since the plant blooms but once in its lifetime, there aren't too many maguey blossoms available, even for esoteric experimenters.

"Fresh Waters" (Soft Drinks)

The so-called *aguas frescas* or fresh waters, made from infusions of fruits, flowers and seeds, are a part of Mexican tradition. Some are even pre-Hispanic in origin, like the *chia,* a tiny seed from one of the many varieties of sage. High in proteins and oils, and negligible in weight and bulk, it served Aztec messengers as K-rations. The drink is made by soaking the seeds in water until each one produces a gelatinous case. Lime or lemon juice and sugar are then added to the water. Chia adds only a delicate, almost imperceptible flavor to the resulting beverage, but it offers a change from the usual lemonade and tremendous boost in nutritive value. Chia, like the following three, can be purchased in Mexico, and taken back to use at home many months, even years, later.

The most beautiful, and possibly the tastiest, of the aguas frescas is *jamaica,* made from the dried red calyxes that surround the yellow blooms of *Hibiscus sabdariffa,* a small relative of the showy ornamental hibiscus. The pinkish purple liquid that results from steeping the red calyxes is an invitation to drink. About the nearest approximation to its flavor is cranberry juice, diluted and debittered.

Then there is *tamarindo,* made from the fleshy pod of the tamarind tree. Like the jamaica blossoms, the pods are brought to a boil and left to steep for several hours. The liquid is then sieved and sugar added to taste. It may be made up and stored as a concentrate for instant mixing — into a pale, russet colored beverage that has a flavor reminiscent of dried apricots.

Arrayán is the least known of this tasty trio of take-homes. Very similar in appearance to large currants, the fruit can often be found in candy stores where crystallized fruit is sold, and eaten as is, or ground, soaked and sieved.

These all make excellent sherbet bases and are commercially prepared as such in Mexico. They can also serve as novel mixes for vodka, especially tamarindo and jamaica.

Fruits

The diversity of climatic zones and altitudes ranging from sea level to high tableland means a happy home somewhere in the Mexican Republic for almost every fruit. Some foreign fruits have become so acclimated that they are thought of as native: the mango, for instance. It made several stops before arriving in Mexico from the East Indies in the early 1800's. Most popular is the *mango de Manila,* pale yellow and thickly fleshed around a large flat seed. Lately, hybridization has created delicious variants, such as the *mango petacón,* larger and thicker with a pink flushed green skin and orange yellow pulp.

Other fruits are so identified with Mexico that they are known both at home and abroad by their Indian names, like the sapotes, for the most part unrelated botanically. The designation *tzapotl,* as part of a compound name, was applied by pre-Conquest peoples to all sweet, soft-fleshed fruits. The four most popular varieties are the black, the white, the *borracho* (drunken), and the *chicozapote.*

The "black" sapote (referring to the pulp; the skin is a dark green) is related to the persimmon and similar in consistency. It is usually prepared by removing the skin and seeds, then mashing the pulp together with sugar and orange juice. Orange or tangerine liqueur may be substituted.

With a pale green skin and delicately flavored sweet white pulp, the white sapote is a cousin to the citrus fruits. The drunken sapote is yellow inside and out and derives its name from the slightly fermented taste of the pulp. It is usually just peeled and eaten as is. The chicozapote is the fruit of the chicle tree, the sap of which is the source of chewing gum. A much smaller fruit than the others, it is a light brown color inside and out and it, too, is just peeled and eaten.

Another of the group is the *mamey-sapote,* called simply mamey. This elongated oval fruit has a hard shell and the flesh is a deep apricot color. There are many more fruits in Mexico that have to be tasted to be believed: the brillant pink *pitahaya;* the pale green, deep yellow, and wine colored *tunas,* all edible "cactus apples;" other so-called "apples" are the several species of annona, the most flavorful being the *chirimoya* or "custard apple."

Frying

While Mexican food derives some of its distinctive flavor from the extensive use of frying as a cooking method, the use of oils and fats in the following recipes has been curtailed, bowing to the U.S. preference for low cholesterol foods. As a matter of interest, in recent years vegetable oils — sunflower and safflower principally — have supplanted lard in Mexican kitchens.

Herbal Teas

Herbal teas have a long and honored history in Mexico. Their use has persisted to the present day, particularly in rural areas where home remedies are the rule. The use of such teas, of course, has not been and is not confined to Mexico. It is simply that there are more of them in Mexico due to the rich variety of plant life, and because the pre-Hispanic high culture civilizations experimented with plants and classified their properties to the level of a true pharmacology.

Some of the more popular remedies in common use today are, for instance, dried bougainvillea flowers which make a delicately flavored, rose tinted tea good for calming a persistent cough. Orange blossom tea is supposed to do the same, and even attenuate the symptoms of whooping cough. Seville orange leaves brewed with a few cloves make an excellent and flavorful digestive aid as well as being a gentle soporific. For multiple therapy, according to the native pharmacopeia, fresh spearmint and lemon grass brewed together will ease stomach disorders, treat any possible fever, and soothe the nerves. An infusion of the magnolia blossom is reputed to tame a tachycardia into a gentle rhythmic beat — in fact, the Aztec name for magnolia means "heart regulator."

Corn silk tea is a universal remedy for kidney problems where a diuretic is indicated but, to be effective, the corn silk must be dried slowly in the shade. Then, supposedly, it will even dissolve gallstones. Major ailments have their herbal tea remedies, too, with specifics for stomach ulcers, epilepsy, high blood pressure, hormonal imbalances, hemorrhages, even cancer. And should there still be doubters, a highly respected Mexican botanist said: *When the effect commonly ascribed to a plant is not achieved, it is likely that neither the plant nor the procedures for using it have been studied sufficiently. . . .It is rare that the Indians erred concerning the uses of medicinal plants.*

Jícama

Gaining popularity abroad, the globular root of this plant, peeled and sliced, is a fresh crisp addition to any salad or refreshing alone. Interestingly enough, while it is a legume, it is the root which is edible. However, the seeds in its pod may be of future interest since they contain rotenone, a substance which is an effective insecticide.

Limes

Both of the principal varieties of limes (Persian and key limes, as they are known in the United States) used in Mexico are now widely available. Lemons, therefore, should not be used as substitutes for limes in any of the recipes given here. Unless fresh lime juice is specified, bottled or canned unsweetened lime juice may be used.

Tomatoes and "Tomatillos"

In Mexico, the names used for tomato and tomatillo are *jitomate* (red) and *tomate* (green). Derived from the Nahuatl words *xitomatl* and *tomatl,* the similarity would imply that these are fruits of the same or closely related plants, which is not the case. While both are members of the Solanaceae family, which also includes among others, potatoes, chiles, and tobacco, they belong to different genera. The husk-like covering of the green tomato places it in the genus *Physalis,* while the red tomato belongs to the genus *Lycopersicum.* Green tomatoes have always been a favorite with country folk since they grow wild or nearly so in the fields, while the red variety must be cultivated. Where the word "tomatillo" comes from is hard to say. It is certainly not used in Mexico but it is the most common designation on cans of green tomatoes exported (they are not found canned in Mexico), although *tomate verde* may appear.

Tortillas

According to the Maya creation legend, the first successful edition of man was shaped from corn dough, undoubtedly very similar to the *masa* or dough used in making tortillas —a fair indication of the importance of corn-based food in the pre-Hispanic diet. Within the rigid structure of Aztec society, where self-control was the keynote, tortilla consumption was regimented. The average citizen ate two tortillas twice a day, together with his beans and chile. The per-meal ration for children was one-half a tortilla at age three, a whole one for ages 4 to 5, and one and a half at six years.

Corn tortillas have continued to serve as the daily bread of most Mexicans. The masa or dough is made of dried field corn, heated and soaked in a mild solution of limewater for 24 hours. The softened kernels are then ground on a *metate* or stone slab. At this point, the masa is also the basis for gruels and tamales. After grinding, the tortillas are shaped, preferably by hand, and then baked on a very hot griddle. Tortillas can be white, yellow or blue, depending upon the color of the corn, and the diameter of the handmade product can vary from three to 12 inches, according to use and local custom. There are also "fat" tortillas, *gorditas,* and *pellizcadas* or pinched ones, one side being pinched all over before baking.

The flour tortilla was, of course, a late arrival, after the Spaniards brought wheat. Its most widespread use in Mexico is in the north where wheat grows better than corn. Outside of Mexico, corn tortillas tend to resemble flexible cardboard, and really become palatable only after they have been fried for tacos, enchiladas, etc. There are exceptions, of course. Flour tortillas, however, are good on either side of the border.

Vinegar

Commercial rice vinegar is a good mild vinegar for use where indicated in the following recipes, but vinegars are easily made at home. A very good one is pineapple vinegar, made as follows: Use a two-quart glass container with a stopper which does not fit too tightly — a little air accelerates the process. Put in the peel of a small pineapple with some of the flesh sticking to it, six cups of water and one-third cup dark brown sugar. Allow to stand in a sunny place. In two to three weeks a "mother" or rubbery film will begin to form on the surface. Taste the vinegar for acidity and if acceptable (if not sufficently tart, check again in a week), strain off up to two cups into a glass jar. Cap tightly and keep to use as needed. Add more water to the liquid remaining in the brewing bottle; it is a never ending process.

Author's Note: The foregoing section of "Notes on Ingredients" was contributed by my good friend and editor Virginia B. de Barrios, a longtime student of Mexican food. She also cooks.

Esta primera edición de MEMORIES OF MEXICO AND RECIPES, TOO por Dorothy Weeks se terminó de imprimir el día 15 de Julio de 1983 en los talleres de Laboratorio Lito Color, S. A., Av. Pacífico 312, 04330 México, D. F., constando de 5,000 ejemplares.